For Douglas (Coptic-e...) woman,
The Painter's Eye,
fraternally Elisew

THE PAINTER'S EYE

Books by MAURICE GROSSER

PAINTING IN PUBLIC

THE PAINTER'S EYE

the Painter's Eye

BY

Maurice Grosser

RINEHART & COMPANY, INC.
NEW YORK TORONTO

PRINTED IN THE UNITED STATES OF AMERICA

Affectionately to

JANE, SALLY

AND

MARGARET ANN

ACKNOWLEDGMENT

The author takes this occasion to thank a few among the many friends who have helped him in preparing this book: the painters, Marcel Duchamp, Isabel Bishop, Reginald Marsh and John Koch; the scientists, Allen Holden of the Bell Telephone Laboratories, Charles Kumins of the Interchemical Laboratories and Dr. Herbert Ives, formerly of the Bell Telephone Laboratories, now retired; the historians, Dr. Garrett Mattingly of Columbia University, Dr. C. Dewitt Eldridge of George Washington University, S. Foster Damon of Brown University, George Leslie Stout of the Worcester Art Museum and Donald Gallup of the Yale University Library; the restorers, Murray Pease of the Metropolitan Museum of New York and William Suhr of the Frick Collection; Miss Pearl Moeller of the library of the Museum of Modern Art of New York and the librarians of the Library of Congress, the New York Public Library, the Chattanooga Public Library, and the Library of the University of Denver, who have been so courteous and helpful; Basil Petrov of M. Knoedler and Co., R. Kirk Askew Jr. of Durlacher Brothers, Kurt Valentine of Buchholz gallery, Alexander Jolas of the Hugo gallery, Julien Levy, Miss Betty Parsons and the Pierre Matisse Gallery; for literary counsel, Frank Daniel of the Atlanta Journal, John Marshall of the Rockefeller Foundation, Virgil Thomson and Miss Peggy Glanville-Hicks of the New York Herald Tribune, Miss Nina Garsoian, Miss Jean Dulebohn, and Isaac Watkins.

CONTENTS

ILLUSTRATIONS

Sixteen pages of photographs follow page 164 of the text.

ILLUSTRATIONS

THE PAINTER'S EYE

CHAPTER ONE

THE PORTRAIT

If torn from all we hold most dear
The tedious moments slowly roll,
Can Music's tenderest accents cheer
The silent grief that melts the soul?
Or can the Poet's boasted art,
The healing balm of peace impart?
Ah! no. 'Tis only Painting's power
Can soothe the sad, the pensive hour,
Can bring the much loved form to view,
In features exquisitely true.
The sparkling eye, the blooming face,
The shape adorned with every grace,
To Nature's self scarce yield the doubtful strife,
Swell on the ravished sight and ask the gift of life.

From the preface to an English color merchant's catalogue entitled *A Treatise on Ackerman's Superfine Watercolors, With Directions How to Prepare and Use them* (London, 1801).

THE PAINTER'S EYE

There hangs in the Metropolitan Museum of New York a painting by Veronese of a youth with a greyhound. The boy's hose are a wonderful, impossible green, a green that is almost black and hardly green at all—perhaps Veronese's celebrated green gone bad, as it so often did. The picture itself is a magnificent piece of painting. It is none the less a portrait, ordered and sat for, paid for and resembling—just such a portrait as were so many of the finest works of art of former times. Today, we have more fine painters than we know what to do with. Yet few of the portraits of our time are works of art; few are even works of passable skill. It might be interesting to inquire why the portrait is now so fallen, looking at the question from the painter's point of view.

The subject of the Pre-Renaissance painters had been God, His laws and works. The subject of the later painters was man. The painter of devotional pictures in Renaissance times was often embarrassed by the limitations of this subject, for he was forced to portray even the divine personages as believable human beings. But with the variety, dignity, and grandeur of man as his subject, the painter was at home. Man he knew, and painting from the Renaissance thereafter is crammed with every possible form of humanity—as pagan gods, monks, soldiers, angels, whores, kings, princes, ladies, beggars, saints and children—painted with every conceivable form of background or scenery, clothes or trappings. But it is the people themselves, not the scenes they occupy, which were the painter's subject. His pictures were large, his equipment cumbersome; he worked principally indoors. The landscape and architecture in his pictures were painted after sketches or from memory and have only a minor, a decorative importance. A few painters like Correggio made actual stage-set models for the backgrounds of their important pictures and peopled them with small wax figures so that their representation of architecture, perspective, light and cast-shadow might be more convincing. But even in these pictures, the painter's subject was still the people he depicted. Landscape and architecture were only the background for their living, and still-life only what they used and wore.

With such a subject the painter's simplest problem was the painting of a single person, and a portrait was the commonest thing he would be asked to do. Today the portrait painter is held in low esteem. Professional portrait painting has become a branch of commercial art like landscape architecture or interior decoration, in which success depends more on rich connections and social abilities than on any special painting talent. But the painter of those times was not thought less of for painting portraits. In fact, portraits were what he was expected to do. Since human variety was the painter's natural subject, any man of any character whatsoever could be painted, and anyone who could afford it sat for his portrait. All great families possessed private picture galleries for the portraits which explained the family's importance and incidentally defined its character. A gallery with a great many children's portraits, for example, is the mark of a family dominated by powerful women. A mother is always proudest of her children while they are still young and pretty and dependent, and it is like this, if she can, that she will have them remembered. In the same way, a gallery of the portraits of the mature and old is the mark of an ambitious family well aware of the historical importance of its line. For portraits are expensive, and laborious to sit for. A member of such a family would wait to be painted until he had done something worth recording—unless, of course, he was heir to a throne—or at least until he was old enough to show his character and promise. The sitter was not expected to charm but to awe. Today we are constantly astonished at the brutal and unflattering character the painters of the fifteenth, sixteenth, and seventeenth centuries were permitted to attribute even to the most powerful princes.

There were countless portraits to be done. Kings had their pictures painted to make their faces known to their subjects. The innumerable portraits, all copied one from another like those of Philip IV of Spain by Velasquez, furnished decoration and splendor for the royal palaces, and were distributed as marks of friendship and favor to noblemen and to other royal houses. Portraits of marriageable princes and princesses were exchanged as a preliminary to a proposal of marriage (just as a portrait of Mlle. Omorphi on a snuffbox proposed her to Louis XV for a less formal arrangement). Relatives sent their portraits to relatives just as today we send photographs, and the private portrait gallery served to keep family records and entertain visitors just as the daguerreotype album did in Victorian times. If one remembers how busy portrait photographers are kept at the present time, we cannot be astonished at the enormous number of portraits the painters formerly turned out. For, before the invention of photography, portrait painting was the one job every painter had to be able to do.

But, common as portrait painting has always been in

the past, I do not believe it has ever been easy. Other painting is done, if not in private, at least in privacy of mind. Portrait painting must be done in public. It is the painter's one public performance, where, like a singer before an audience or an actor on a stage, the painter has an immediate response from his public to the picture he is painting. Here he must deal with the will as well as the person of his sitter. Any kind of painting is difficult enough. Having the painter's client and most captious critic as subject for his picture adds further difficulty. As a result, the portrait is the most hazardous, the most trying on the nerves, and the least certain of success, of any work the painter can undertake. Not only must he paint his sitter, he must convince him as well. And he must entertain him at the same time.

Formerly this was easier. The painter's studio was a general meeting place. Painters did not mind working before an audience. As the painter painted, the friends and visitors could be depended on to keep the sitter awake and entertained. I suppose this must have been the case until very recently indeed, for there is a picture by Fantin-Latour, called *Un Atelier aux Batignolles*, of Manet's studio, where the painter, in his company clothes, is shown at work on a portrait, surrounded and undisturbed by a group of the most famous painters and literary men of his day. But the painter of our time has no such aids. He must entertain his sitter himself. For he has become accustomed to work in the sequestered intimacy of an analyst's alcove, and with the added burden of a patient at all times free to consult the doctor's notes.

With a little training and patience, all this can be dealt with. Painters quickly learn how to chatter automatically even when they are working most seriously. Some even come to enjoy it. The real difficulty is not this. The difficulty is one inherent in the portrait itself. For a portrait is not like any other sort of picture. It is not a simple representation of the sitter, nor does the simple act of painting a man, however well it may be done, necessarily produce a portrait of him. In fact, the portrait seems to depend so little on careful or accurate drawing that wretched and even untrained painters can frequently produce astonishing resemblances. A portrait may be painted well or ill and still succeed. But if it does not present a convincing likeness of the sitter, it is not a successful portrait. In this way it is like caricature. For, like caricature, a portrait is a picture whose unique subject is the resemblance. This resemblance is not in any way the complete image of a man. It is obtained, like caricature, by looking at the man from a special point of view. To get it, a peculiar state of sympathy, of a mysterious and almost magical nature, must be established and maintained between the painter and his sitter. How this is done, nobody, not even the most experienced portrait painter, understands. With some sitters it comes easily. With others it cannot be got at all. Sometimes it is there, and then, for no apparent reason, it will disappear, never to return. If it exists and continues to exist, the portrait will look like the sitter, whether it is painted well or ill. If this state of sympathy cannot be evoked, the portrait, no matter how skillful the painter, will not be resembling nor can it ever be.

This state of sympathy, this psychological nearness, which constitutes the difference between a portrait and any other sort of painting, depends directly on the actual physical interval—the distance in feet and inches—between the painter and his model. And a portrait can be defined as a picture painted at a distance of four to eight feet of a person who is not paid to sit. A picture painted from nearer or farther away is often a recognizable likeness. It can seldom, however, be properly called a portrait. The characteristic quality of a portrait is the peculiar sort of communication, almost a conversation, that the person who looks at the picture is able to hold with the person painted there. This depends on there being depicted on the canvas at the same time both the sitter's soul—or how he feels to himself—and his character—or the part he plays in the outside world. A duality such as this is too difficult for a painter to establish if he works nearer the sitter than four feet, or farther away than eight or nine.

This is by no means as strange as it might first appear. A sitter, or for that matter, anyone at all, has three possible aspects, all completely different. Which one of the three aspects he presents to us depends directly on the distance at which we stand to see him. The measure of this distance is the natural unit which, without ever thinking, we use to measure all the outside world—the height of our own bodies.

At more than thirteen feet away, in other words, at more than twice the height of our own bodies, the human figure can be seen in its entirety as a single whole. At this distance we are scarcely aware of the figure's solid bulk. We see only its outline and proportions. At this distance we can look at a man as if he were a shape cut out of cardboard, as something having no connection with ourselves. For it is largely the sense of space, of solidity, of extension in depth, which two-eyed vision gives for objects near at hand that operates to produce in the observer a feeling of kinship, of sympathy, with the thing observed. At twice its height, all the figure can be seen at once. It can be comprehended at a glance. It can be understood as a unit and a whole. At this distance the figure's posture, its position, its dignity or lack of it, its resistance to the pull of gravity, its relation to the plane on which it stands—in sum, its character—all this is quite easy to understand. At this distance, whatever meaning or feeling the figure may convey is dominated, not by the expression of the features of the face, but by the position of the members of the body. At this distance the painter can look at his model as if he were a tree in a landscape, or an apple in a still-life which, by some unimportant accident, happens to be alive. The sitter's personal warmth does not disturb. The painter can see his model without any personal involvement, and can put him on his canvas as objectively as he pleases. It is from this distance that figure painting is done and mural painter's models are drawn and painted.

Michelangelo and his imitators, of course, do not observe this rule. Their figures are painted as if the model were within touching distance of the painter's hands. But these frescos of the Sistine Chapel and the numberless ceilings of Vasari, of his school and his fellows, are not, strictly speaking, mural painting at all, for they have no backgrounds. Their backgrounds are either painted cornices and niches, or the most perfunctory of clouds and garlands. Real mural painting, like Ghirlandaio's *Birth of the Virgin* or Gozzoli's *Procession of the Magi*, has depth. It has space for its figures to exist in and backgrounds behind them.

The mural painter's figures must not lie flat on the surface of the wall like a bas-relief. They must be pushed back well within the space which the picture pretends to contain. To accomplish this the painter must draw his figures as if he were standing at a distance of at least twice their height.

But four to eight feet is the portrait distance. At this distance the painter is near enough so that his eyes have no trouble in understanding the sitter's solid forms, yet he is far enough away so that the foreshortening of the forms presents him no real problem. Here, at the normal distance of social intimacy and easy conversation, the sitter's soul begins to appear. Since it is the soul, or rather a nice balance of soul and character, which forms the subject of a portrait, this is the distance from which portraits must be painted. Nearer than three feet, within touching distance, the soul is far too much in evidence for any sort of disinterested portraiture. This is the sculptor's, not the painter's, working distance. The sculptor must stand near enough his model to be able to judge the forms by sense of touch. Besides, the sculptor has no problems of perspective. His statue has no background. He has not the painter's problem of giving an equal aspect to near and distant objects. Only when the painter does a still-life can he work as close to his model as the sculptor does. Then, by limiting the depth in his picture, and by bringing the background close behind his still-life objects, he can paint the background as another of the objects in the picture, and neglect perspective. By this device, the painter can sometimes treat his still-life objects as if they were models for sculpture and paint them from within touching distance. But people he cannot treat so. At touching distance, the problems of foreshortening make the business of painting itself too difficult. At touching distance, the painter must deal with the distortions caused by the closeness of the sitter to his eye; and the almost insoluble problem of depicting with equal detail, precision and convincingness, the close-up, solid figure and the more distant, flatter background. Moreover, at touching distance, the sitter's personality is too strong. The influence of the model on the painter is too powerful, too disturbing to the artist's necessary detachment, touching distance being not the position of visual rendition, but of motor reaction, of some physical expression of sentiment, like fisticuffs, or the various acts of love.

If the distance from his model is important to the painter, so also is the size which he depicts him. Whatever we see in nature appears large or small according to its distance. But because we see with two eyes, we can estimate this distance, and correct our impression of the object by the estimate; and thus we come to understand the object's real dimensions. The size of any object is the first thing we are obliged to know about it. On its size depends how we must treat the object, or how it may treat us. Any object which is to be used by the hands, or understood by the mind, or comprehended by the emotions, must first be compared with our one basic unit of physical measurement—a man's own size. Anything too large or too small to be measured by that unit, like the distance of Sirius to the Sun, or the dimensions of a molecule, cannot be comprehended directly; to be understood at all, it must first be translated as if from another language. Actually, such translation is impossible. Light years and microns are both logical constructions and can be immediately derived one from the other by a simple multiplication. Neither of them has anything in common with the mile, which is arrived at by quite a different sort of construction, not logical at all—how long it will take us to walk the mile and how tired we will feel when we have done so. Translation from the Galactic or the Microscopic to the Human vernacular can be made in terms of only one sentiment—a tiresome, hypnotic awe.

Within the human scale, there is easy comprehension and endless variety. We know that certain things have certain sizes. If we see them larger or smaller, we feel the difference at once. Any object, an egg or a head, painted larger or smaller than we are accustomed to seeing it, has for us a new and different meaning; it depends on how our eyes are actually adjusted to focus on the picture, and how our eyes should be adjusted to see the object if it were at the distance its unusual size implies. There is as well the shock of seeing something depicted larger or smaller than we know it could possibly be.

Today we are somewhat inclined to forget that objects, like hands or horses, have only one proper and normal size which cannot be changed without changing their meaning, because we have become accustomed to seeing such objects enlarged to gigantic proportions by projection on a moving picture screen. We forget that what we see there is only a photographic image. It is neither the objects themselves, nor even a drawing of them. The surface of the image is constructed optically by rays of light, without the use of hands, of brushes or muscular tensions. There is nothing about the image which would indicate its size. But if this enlargement, this projected photograph, were traced on the screen by hand and then viewed by ordinary light, the image would no longer have the vague dimensions of a photograph. Our two eyes would tell us how big the picture is and how far we are from the screen on which it is drawn. Our muscular senses would inform us of the tensions felt by the hand that traced it. We would at once perceive the difference between the size of the image and the size we know the object itself to be. This is what happens when we look at any painting. A heroic figure—say, one of the Sibyls of the Sistine Chapel—seen from no matter how far away remains a heroic figure still. Our eyes triangulate the distance and make the necessary calculations. We are at once aware not only how much bigger the figure is than life, but also than ourselves.

In this question of size lies one of the unavoidable inefficiencies of present-day instruction. Students of the history of art are accustomed to see almost all the pictures they study as prints or lantern slides—either the size of the page of a book or of a projection screen—and all, consequently, considerably falsified. It is, of course, as impossible to show the pictures in their proper size as it would be to make accurate color reproductions of them. But, the size of a picture, and the size of the objects in it as well, are critically important in determining the picture's character, its use and its effect.

A large picture must have more detail than can be had simply by enlarging a small one. So, to a painter at work, the size of his picture is an immediate consideration, because the size of his picture determines the amount of detail that will be required and consequently the amount of painstaking work the painter will be required to do. The painter stands as he paints not more than three feet from his canvas. The finished picture must look well from the distance at which it was intended to be viewed. But it must also remain interesting when seen from the distance at which the painter stood to paint it. Thus, a small picture enlarged without enough detail added to permit a close inspection will appear empty. This is one of the reasons why contemporary mural painting is so seldom satisfactory. Murals, in this country at any rate, are generally planned as small sketches, and as small sketches, accepted by the purchaser. Enlarged without change to the size of the wall, they will necessarily come out thin and over-simple. The spectator sees at once, by comparing their size to their poverty of detail, that they are only enlargements.

All painters from Giotto and Michelangelo to Pavel Tchelitchew and Georgia O'Keeffe, are aware of the emotional implications of size and play with it constantly, even to the extent of varying the scale of sizes in the same picture. There is, for example, a Rembrandt self-portrait in the Frick Collection where the painter's head and body are of one size while the left hand, reaching forward, is considerably larger. The difference of the size of the hand from the rest of the picture is exactly the difference a person standing within four feet of a seated figure would see, and gives the spectator the disconcerting sensation of being within touching distance of the end of Rembrandt's nose.

The effect painters more commonly employ is a simple change of size—painting things larger or smaller than one expects to find them. It is, in fact, a general rule in painting not to paint anything, especially not a face or a near-by object, in the commonplace size of three fourths as large as life. The problem of enlarging or reducing from the size which is easy, normal or expected gives an added difficulty of the act itself of painting which the spectator feels as an added excitement—exactly like the tension a musician can produce by singing high or by playing an instrument in a difficult range.

A number of painters of our time have tried, by great enlargement, or by painting very close to the sitter, to produce an effect similar to the close-up of the films which, to the painter, is the film's most striking invention. The motion picture of itself is somewhat weak in emotional appeal. Its scenes have no natural continuity. The people it portrays are only photographs and have not the solidity, warmth, or power of projection of living actors moving on a stage. Producers have found that background music, if it is neutral enough not to distract the spectator's attention, will unite the film's uneven sequences and, by its harmonic richness, compensate in part for the human warmth these photographs of actors cannot furnish; and that the emotional impact of a living, present, person can be in part supplied by bringing the actors' lips apparently within three inches of our own. Painting has no need for background music. It has its own intensity and needs no added warmth. But almost every painter of the present day has experimented with effects of intimacy provided by the close-up head.

It was, I believe, the late Christian Bérard who first used the close-up systematically in painting. He showed in Paris in 1927 a group of over-life-size portraits which were astonishing in their intimacy, and while unmistakably resembling, had very little of the sitters' specific outer appearance. Intimacy and lack of specific characterization are natural to this kind of close-up portrait. Intimacy increases as the painter draws nearer the sitter. And when characterization is enlarged, or outer character is seen from too close, it can only become caricature, and hence must be avoided. Thus, the close-up portrait, by its very want of any characterization save that of the painter's own style, is likely to portray not the sitter, but the painter reflected in the sitter's face, and to produce an effect of intimacy, not with the sitter, but with the painter himself.

So, wonderful as some of these pictures are, they can scarcely be called real portraits. They are pictures of what the painter before his model feels like to himself, rather than an objective representation of the sitter's real appearance. Most of the pictures we commonly think of as portraits are painted from the conventional distance of four to eight feet—the larger distance being taken when the whole of a seated figure is to be shown.

Full-length portraits, like Gainsborough's *Blue Boy* or Sargent's *Madame X*, are done on a somewhat different system. The painter places his canvas on a level with his sitter and he himself stands some thirteen or fourteen feet away. He walks forward to the canvas when he wishes to put on a stroke of paint, and paints with brushes three to six feet long to minimize his walking. For when one brush stroke has been made, he must go back to his vantage point before deciding upon the next. Standing at this distance of about thirteen or fourteen feet, the painter can judge his work from the position a spectator will take to view the finished picture. By this means also, the painter can avoid the violent and apparently false perspective—the appearance of a tilted floor—which working too close and with too wide a visual angle would give. All this, however, is only for laying in the picture. The actual painting of the head, hands, and the details of costume is done from the accustomed distance of four to eight feet.

Within this conventional painting distance the painting of a portrait becomes a simple tug-of-war: who has the more power, the painter or the sitter. (Or rather, more precisely, which of the two has a greater *mana*, using *mana* as the anthropologists do, for the concept of the sum of a person's magical powers.) The sitter's mana depends on his wealth, his age, his social position, his energies, the quality of his intelligence, and his own secret estimate of the value of each one of these things. The painter's mana depends on his confidence in his own skill, his reputation in the professional world of painting, and on the size and social importance of his clientele. If the painter's mana is stronger, he is undisturbed by the sitter's presence, and the sitter will be seen from the outside. In this case the portrait will come out a picture, not of a soul, but of a character, and will be as well painted as the painter's talent can effect. But since the sitter never sees himself from the outside, there is the danger for the painter that his client will not accept, or even recognize, the character he has been assigned. If, on the other hand, the sitter is the stronger, the painter will be overmastered and the portrait will become an inside view of the sitter. Here the painter is forced to see the sitter through the sitter's own eyes and to paint the sitter's soul—this lambent energy that only its possessor ever sees—rather than the sitter's character—the way in which he appears to the outside world. Pictures of the soul are, generally speaking, unsatisfactory, even when attenuated, as in Landseer's dogs or Watts' *Hope*. Excess of intimacy is endurable only for a short time and under special conditions. When the painter is overmastered, he loses his technical freedom, and however much the sitter himself may be pleased with the result, such a portrait is likely to be ill painted as a picture; and as a characterization, it will certainly be weak.

It is the sitter's insuperable mana which makes the many portraits of Marie Antoinette by Madame Vigée-Lebrun so unworthy of this excellent painter. As Queen of France, the sitter might have been handled. But Marie Antoinette, unlike her predecessors, Maria Theresa of Spain and Marie Leczinska, was more than Queen of France. She was also the leader of the most fashionable and self-sufficient social set in Paris. In her quality of Europe's most exclusive hostess, she was, for her painter, impossible. In all these pictures the velvet is beautiful, the carriage of the body gracious and superb; but the head above is a monument of vagueness and charm.

The sitter, of course, is always strong. None but the rich and powerful order portraits. Most important of all, the sitter pays. And, as far as I know, there is no way of making a sitter accept, or at any rate hang, a portrait, no matter how well painted, with which he is not pleased. So, the sitter has always an initial advantage. But the painter can also be strong, even stronger than the sitter; if, for example, he is protected by an effective professional association, such as the guilds of former times; or if the painter's social position is so negligible that he can be regarded as a workman whose opinions, even if expressed in painting, are a matter of no importance to his client; or if, on the contrary, the painter's social position in the sitter's own world is so secure that the painter can do as he pleases; or even if he is simply older than his client and can impress him with a greater experience and knowledge of the world than his sitter yet possesses.

It is the particular qualities of character needed by the painter for this tug-of-war which explains why portraits of the rich and royal of our own time, satisfactory as they may be as likenesses, are so invariably dull. The painter of today has no professional support to sustain him in the presence of these awesome sitters. The royal or millionaire client must choose his painter, not from among the good ones, but from among the ones who are strong enough to face him down and get his likeness, painters whose social position and worldly experience are on a par with the client's own. These qualifications seldom make good painters.

The early Italian portrait painters like Ghirlandaio probably used their guilds to give them weight and resistance to their sitters; Titian and Rubens were stars as much in the public eye as movie actors today. John Singer Sargent belonged to the class of the socially secure, and so did Reynolds. Whatever Reynolds may have lacked in ducal favor was made up by the intellectual distinction of belonging to the Literary Club along with Johnson, Garrick and the other wits. Velasquez, who is reported never to have opened his mouth in the presence of a sitter, was probably regarded by his royal clients as a workman of no more social importance than a good gardener or pastry cook. Degas used another trick. He was celebrated for being the most disagreeable man in Paris. That, to begin with, was an enormous advantage. He also generally arranged his painting distances so as to be out of range of the sitter's soul. Most of his portraits seem to have been painted from at least ten feet away.

It is easiest for a painter to paint things the size he sees them—the size they would occupy on his canvas if it were transparent and he were looking through it at the objects he is painting. If a painter is standing ten feet from his model and his canvas is at the convenient painting distance of about three feet, the model will automatically be drawn at about one third of actual size—unless there is reason to do otherwise. The size of the figures in Degas' portraits would indicate that they were painted at a distance of ten feet or more. At times Degas also painted from photographs and did not have to face his sitter at all. Often he painted his social inferiors—jockeys, dancers, washerwomen; but these last cannot be classed as portraits. The models were probably paid; with the paid model, the problem of the portrait and its tug-of-war does not arise. The fact of being paid erases the sitter's mana, and the painter alone has power. Unless, of course, the painter is painting his model as an excuse or gambit or prelude for love—which case we need not bother with. Undertaken in this expectation, the picture is generally painted from as close as possible, and seldom, if ever, is carried beyond the first sitting.

CHAPTER TWO

THE LIKENESS

> In speaking of likeness in portrait painting Wilkie once said to me that "it was well to increase the beauty of the complexion and give the appearance of youth, as this in a measure compensated for the warmth of life and motion."
>
> Thomas Sully, *Hints to Young Painters*

Nobody knows what he looks like. He knows what he feels like inside and that is all. Even when he looks at himself in a mirror, he arranges his face to fit his inside feelings, or else carefully refrains from seeing it. The glimpse a painter can provide of the outside aspect of this vivid flame each of us knows himself to be is what makes sitting for a portrait such a fascinating business. This is why the portrait painter is as awe-inspiring to his sitter—and as ludicrous—as a fortune teller, and why the painter and the sitter so often find each other so difficult to support and so impossible to forgive.

Whatever form the disagreement between the sitter and the painter may take, and whatever its outcome may be, it is always about the likeness—which soul, which interior life, of all the various interior lives the sitter may possess, shall be ascribed to him; which one of the various aspects of the sitter's soul the portrait shall be made to represent. This likeness must not only be one that is possible; it must also be one that is becoming to the sitter and to his station. The choice requires, on the painter's part, considerable tact and knowledge of the world. So that the resemblance—which means the exterior aspect of an appropriate interior life—is something which the camera, or at any rate the still camera, contrary to a most widespread popular belief, is only by accident ever able to obtain.

This resemblance in a portrait or a photograph is a sort of symbolic representation of the sitter's personality. Or rather it is a summation of it. For the personality never remains still, but is fluid and in constant change. The painter, by observing the sitter over a certain length of time, is able to extract out of the flux of personality an average, and can present this average as a convincing enough resemblance. This is why a portrait can never be painted in less than three or four sittings. The movie camera, by taking in sequence a series of photographs of an actor, can record a section of the flux of his personality, and can present the sequence of this flux as a consistent likeness. The movie camera, too, has this advantage, that the actor, to make it easier, has already been typed and stylized by conventions of plot and make-up. The moving picture camera is, of course, a mechanical and not a human eye, so that the resemblance it obtains is only what the actor looks like to other moving picture cameras, and very seldom what he looks like to ourselves when we meet him face to face.

But the still camera is not capable of recording even this sort of resemblance. The still camera's shutter is instantaneous; it cannot photograph duration. It does not represent nature, it immobilizes it. Its picture of a wave looks like a crumpled sheet of tin, not like the liquid motion we know the wave to be. Of the wave itself the camera can record only the wave's cross section as immobilized in time. In the same way, from the sitter's flux of personality the still camera can extract only a section minutely thin. This cross section is never, except by the rarest of accidents, the representative summation of personality which is called a resemblance.

Besides this, the sitter, poised waiting for the camera's click, is not himself; he is not inside his own mind, leading his own life and thinking his own thoughts. But with his mind a blank, the sitter accepts the impress of the personality of the photographer; so that the picture is most likely to come out looking like the man who snapped the shutter. Even movie actors must take this into consideration. To assure herself a consistent screen personality, Greta Garbo insisted on being photographed always by the same camera man. And Marlene Dietrich, in changing camera men, changed her screen personality. But this last is not ordinarily the case. The public character, the actor as well as the politician, usually knows how to offer the camera his stylized and agreed-upon caricature, and never the fluid surface of his soul. In fact it is the easy and confident employment of this caricature personality that is the distinguishing mark of the class known to professional and publicity circles as "The Big Time." Outside this small class, however, it is a general rule that in having a picture taken, if you expect to like it, you must pick out the photographer whom you would least mind resembling.

We perceive the flux of a man's personality chiefly through the play of the features. But an assemblage of the features will not, alone, produce a resemblance. And the portrait painter who sets out to copy, no matter how carefully, a set of features, will get nowhere. The police use a system of classifying faces according to a set of standard types of features—a long nose, narrow eyes, full lips, cleft chin and so on—which is supposed to work perfectly for identifying criminals who have already been classified. There have been frequent accounts in the public press of how, by assembling on the oval outline of a head the types of features a criminal is reported by witnesses to possess, the portrait of an unknown criminal can be drawn which is resembling enough for him to be recognized by a man in the street. I do not believe this is possible. The features, in themselves, do not contain the resemblance. In fact, the features, as actual entities, do not even exist. They are only verbal abstractions, the convenient names we give to the most mobile parts of the mask or to the most complex joinings of the planes that compose the head. It is by indicating the planes and forms of the head itself and not by drawing the features one by one that the painter arrives at his description of character. He obtains his resemblance by using the quite abstract tensions, pulls and pushes, and mutual distortions of his lines and shapes, to represent something of the pulls and pushes and mutual distortions of the planes and forms of the sitter's head and body. It is only by the interplay of these tensions of lines, planes and masses that character is, or ever can be, expressed.

Each particular combination of lines, planes and masses—in art as well as in nature—has for us a particular meaning. Let us say, for example, that a tree, a real tree in a field, leans to the left. A slight swelling of the ground at its base indicates the position of an important root. If the swelling is to the left, the weight of the tree is pushing the root into the ground. If the swelling is to the right, the tree is pulling against the root, pulling it out of the ground. These we feel as two quite different things, as different as the idea—or the feel—of pushing a car is from the idea—or feel—of lifting a weight. Our muscular senses are elaborately aware of these thrusts and tensions. It is the sympathetic muscular sensation in our own bodies of these thrusts and tensions, and our translation of them in terms of our own emotions, which we interpret as the character of the person we have before us. Because each particular arrangement of the masses of a face or of a body, either in life or on a canvas, by affecting our muscular senses, gives us the knowledge of how our own face would feel if we twisted it into that particular configuration, or of how our own body would feel if it assumed the posture that we see, and what particular emotion or character or sentiment would cause us so to grimace or stand. Thus by using combinations of lines and shapes and masses, and the motor and emotional meanings they have for us (and no such combination is without some such meaning) the painter can describe and make us feel the character of the resemblance he has seen. But exactly how he accomplishes it, not even the painter himself more than dimly understands.

The soul which forms the basis for this resemblance (I am speaking, of course, of the mortal, not the immortal soul—of the interior life, if you prefer) changes character according to the age of its possessor. Almost uncharacterized in childhood, it hardens in youth to display the basic traits of family, descent and race. In middle life it reflects the ambitions of the various groups among which its possessor moves. In old age it is a record of his peculiar fatigues, sins and accomplishments. When we speak of the unself-consciousness of a child we mean nothing more than the self-sufficiency of a well-ordered biological machine running at full speed. The soul of middle years is more mercurial than this, less confident, and is continually being subjected to outside interferences. In old age the soul is again held firm by the rigidity of the past.

The portrait painter's commonest problem is the sitter of middle years. Painting a child is rather a problem of invention and improvisation than of portraiture—how to work rapidly enough to get something done in the short time the painter can hold the child's attention, and how to remember, fill out, and invent a resemblance when his attention can no longer be retained. Painting children is not easy. For here the painter is not only the disinterested observer who records his sitter's character, and the sympathetic friend who responds to the warmth of his sitter's inmost feelings; he is the tyrant nurse as well who keeps him still. Even Goya, I should imagine from the children's portraits of his I have seen, had trouble with this sort of portraiture. His children have none of the precise characterization of his other portraits. They seem, in their wistful vagueness, more like children remembered in their absence than like the noisy, temperamental actuality the painter invariably encounters after his first sitting.

Painting children is easy in one respect. There is no quarrel with the sitter about resemblance. The painter and the sitter inhabit different worlds, and how the painter sees and depicts him is, to the child, completely unimportant. Besides, the child is so little individualized, the traits of its character so subtly defined and so difficult to see, that parents will accept any resemblance at all provided it is not an unpleasant one. Old age, too, is easy—or else impossible—easy if the sitter, along with his years, has also acquired dignity and pride in his experience and accomplishments. But if he is envious of youth and aping it, he can only be caricatured; he cannot be painted. In this case the painter is required to deform his aging sitter's real appearance and to paint, not what he sees is there, but a stylization of appearance that the sitter believes it necessary to seem to possess. Reassuring as such a picture may be to the vanity of an aging sitter, as a painting it can be of little value. It is a picture of an abstraction, an ideal, and has little connection with the real and tangible world, and to the painter's view and love and memory of it, out of which alone painting can be made.

The same sort of difficulty always arises when the society in which the sitter lives places a high value on some such specific ideal of appearance or of decorum. Here the painter is obliged to stylize his sitter's appearance by assigning to his face the resemblance then in fashion. This fashionable appearance is only an ideal, a generalization, and a surface. Even if the sitter has contrived to assume it, it is neither his appearance when he is off his guard, nor his most interesting aspect as a human being. So that portraits painted under the restrictions of such imposed fashions can be neither humanly true nor very interesting.

The distinguishing mark of the portrait in the grand style—of Titian, Bronzino, Rembrandt, Greco and the like—is the absence of this particular form of stylization of appearance. Portraiture in the grand style, just as the school of painting from which it springs, has as its subject man himself, and not any accidental, fashionable or agreeable stylization of his appearance. Nor is its subject matter man-in-general either. The painter in the grand style does not generalize. The still-life painter paints the particular apple he has before him, not the Platonic apple or appleness. The portrait painter in the grand style has nothing to do with man in general or even with any ideal conception of him. He paints instead a particular man—his sitter as a human being whose essential humanity is different from all other examples of mankind. No stylization of appearance, no fashionable or imposed taste, is allowed to come between the painter and his sitter, to diminish the sitter's natural grandeur as Son of Adam and an immortal soul. Pontormo's toughs, Titian's princes, popes and poets, the poor people of Rembrandt, wear their silks and rags and fustians to show off, not to disguise this human dignity. The *Halbardier* of Pontormo in the Stillman Collection is proud of his butter-yellow doublet with its enormous sleeves. He is prouder still of the man inside it. Bronzino's elegant youth in the Frick, dressed *à l'espagnole* in black, his doublet slashed to show his courage in combat, a medal in his hand to indicate his artistic taste, and his manliness demonstrated by a modest codpiece, has a precise character more striking than any of these fashionable accouterments. And Rembrandt's *Old Woman Cutting Her Nails* in the Metropolitan, as dingily dressed as if the cloth of her dress were dish clouts, has in her uningratiating humanity all the inhuman weight of Mother Earth. But she is still a woman, and a woman different from every other.

If the portraits of the eighteenth century are much less interesting to us than these, it is not because their painters were unskillful. On the contrary, the eighteenth century painters were unbelievably skillful. It is simply that their sitters, like all fashionable Europeans of the time, were conforming to a stylization of appearance and deportment which had its origin in France and dominated all Europe in the eighteenth century. Earlier, from the middle of the sixteenth century through the first years of the seventeenth, the fashions in manners and dress of all Europe had been derived from the manners and dress of the court of Spain—or rather from these manners and costumes as interpreted by the Spaniards in Italy and at the court of France, and by the Spanish governors of the Netherlands. The Spanish *morgue* and ceremoniousness and use of black in costume (it was only Spain, where indigo was easily obtainable, that had a good black dye) were admired and imitated in all the courts of Europe. But by the beginning of the eighteenth century, the dress and manners of the court of France had become the model for the appearance and deportment of all the civilized world.

After the first quarter of the century, travel in Europe had become easy everywhere (except in Spain). Leopold Mozart, as anyone else who needed to, was able to trot his prodigy daughter and his prodigious son from Austria to

France, to England, to Italy, and back again, wherever there was a concert to be given or a fee or a gold watch to be gained. With travel thus made easy, national differences, at least among the upper classes, tended to disappear. Charm was everywhere the keynote of fashion; charm and condescension the distinguishing marks of a gentleman. Conversation, the physical sciences (called natural philosophy) and urbane deportment were everywhere esteemed, so that rogues like Cagliostro, Casanova and the Count of Saint Germain (who taught Louis XVI how to make diamonds) led brilliant lives based only on their entertainment value and plausibility. An international set, very like the millionaire Bohemia of the 1920's, wandered over Europe, visiting in chateaux, courts and army camps, occupied with gambling, society, gallantry and the opera. The rich were very rich, and they could enjoy enormous luxury. Workmanship was good everywhere. The guilds still existed; whatever was made was made to endure. Houses, gardens, furniture, brocade, plate, china, statuary, pictures —all sorts of handmade objects were turned out in great quantities for the consumption of the man of taste. The man of taste of today is the man who knows what to like. But the man of taste of the eighteenth century was the man who knew what to buy. Whatever he bought, his taste was dictated by the taste of the French court. And the French court demanded of everyone, everywhere, of whatever age or condition, a universal appearance of ease, urbanity, and charm.

The costume itself, with its long coats and wigs for the men and full bosoms and powdered hair for the women, seems designed to suppress all individual differences—

even of age—save those of social condition. In plays performed in eighteenth century costumes it is easy enough to distinguish the masters from the servants. But among the masters themselves, it is impossible to tell one from another except by the color of the dress. The stylization of deportment and facial expression was equally complete. Even the "noble savage" of the fashionable philosophers, the *Rénés* and *Atalas* and so on, were supposedly endowed by nature with courtly manners. The unexpected or violent in behavior or appearance was considered "Gothick" (just as music that had drums and cymbals was called "Turkish"). The sitter for a portrait presented himself, not as a human being, but as an actor playing with skill, grace, and decorum the role of a human being. There is, for example, a portrait in the Habsburg Collection by the French painter Duplessis, in which the composer, Gluck, at the harpsichord, his conducting hand in full light, seems to be acting out with sweet authority the part of composer-conductor; or the portrait in the Louvre of Louis XV by Hyacinthe Rigaud, where the king, an enormous man in enormous clothes, is playing with complete conviction the part of "Le Roi de France." The painting of these pictures is incredibly beautiful. But the sitters have been endowed with none of the human profundity that portraits painted at an earlier time possess—Titian's *Aretino*, for example, or Greco's *Inquisitor*. For the subject of these eighteenth century portraits is the sitter's social situation, not his status as a member of the human race. This is not the painter's fault. It is simply that the eighteenth century conventions of proper appearance have come between the painter and his sitter, and have veiled from the painter his sitter's reality as a man—a reality which cannot be subjected to any convention and still retain its full power of projection. Besides, this generalized urbanity established by the French taste is scarcely the human animal's most fascinating aspect. And it is not until these conventions had been shattered by the explosion of the French Revolution that the portrait could again assume, as it did with Goya and David, the intensity of interest and power of communication that the direct depiction of the unstylized human being can give.

The painter of our day has this identical problem to face, and in its most excessive form. The stylization our particular age admires is more silly and more rigid than anything the eighteenth century painter had to deal with. The eighteenth century sitter demanded only to be made gracious and urbane. The present-day sitter must have charm. As a result, the portraits painted today are low in moral tone and deplorable in execution. In spite of the important place portrait painting has always held in the past, and the gainful occupation it has always been, few of the first-rate contemporary painters ever bother with it. The conventions that govern portrait painting today are too narrow to hold their interest. The origin of our stylization of appearance is the moving pictures.

The court at Versailles no longer acts as the source of fashion; in our time it is the studios of Hollywood, the factories of our popular entertainment. "Entertainment," however, is not an accurate name for what the film industry provides. In fact, very few of its films are entertaining in any way. Its audiences do not pay to be amused. They pay instead to sit quietly in darkness and to be tranquilized by seeing passed before their eyes the images of the fulfillment of their most urgent needs—of spending money and of receiving love. Dramatic interest is only an extra ornament added on—like technicolor. The film's essential requirement is to seduce and charm. This seduction, this charm, has many forms but it is always there. It is the make-up without which not even the simplest extra portraying a villain would be allowed to appear before the camera. This mask of charm on an actor's face assures us that he is part of the harmless dream we have paid to see, and not a part of the intrusive and dangerous outside world. This is the stylization that Hollywood has imposed on all its actors—and on all of us as well.

A version of human behavior has a greater influence on our everyday behavior than we commonly suppose. How we actually look or act is not changed by it. What is changed is how we like to think of ourselves as looking, and how we like to think of our effect, and the effect of our charm, on other people. This stylization places an impossible limitation on the painter who paints a portrait today. For his sitter has in mind, as the model he must be made to resemble, not any one human being or even any one human quality, but the general idea of pleasing derived from all the many films the sitter has ever seen. So that the sitter has seldom a simple conception of how he would like to be made to appear. If the sitter's wishes are respected, and the painter endows him with all the kinds of charm he demands, the portrait will come out looking at once like a great many contradictory things. The painter, faced with the necessity of making a matron look at once rich, authoritative and meltingly seductive—everyone, said Gertrude Stein, thinks of himself as a mature young person

—the painter, I say, will probably abandon his scruples, neglect his sitter's real character, and paint her with the official glamour and generalized sex-appeal of a movie actress giving an autograph. The painter despises himself and the work he is paid to do. Consequently serious painters seldom paint portraits. For portraits painted with such a reduced view of the infinite variety of human nature can have little human or artistic value and will, in the future, be of merely documentary interest.

Hollywood is not entirely to blame. The real source of the painter's difficulty is photography. Photography is all about us. We know it too well. We trust it too much. The public has come to believe that the camera's view of nature, not the eye's view or the painter's view, is the true one. A photograph is real, tangible and durable, like an object—not evanescent, like an appearance. And since the movie camera, which is the most convincing of all the devices of photography, never shows a visage without charm, a portrait painted without something of the same seduction cannot be a true representation of nature.

After all, in a way, the public is right. This official charm, this appearance of the anxiety to please, which we see in all films, in all advertisements, on all public faces, has now come to be the recognized outward aspect of the American National Character.

CHAPTER THREE

THE GRAND STYLE

> Shakespere has no heroes; his scenes are occupied only by men.
>
> Samuel Johnson, *Preface to Shakespere*

There is in the Frick Collection a portrait by Hogarth of a Miss Mary Edwards, one of the richest women in England, who is said to have declared her son a bastard in order to get her fortune back again from the noble lord she had married. The lady in Hogarth's picture, with her jewels, her dog and her indulgent smile, is very English. She has not one touch of the continental amenities of appearance. She resembles rather her contemporary *Moll Flanders* as Defoe's moral example might have appeared in one of her prosperous years.

Near this hangs another portrait of an English woman, of the Countess of Clanbrassil, by Van Dyke. Van Dyke's lady is aloof, gracious and perfectly characterized. But unlike Hogarth's sitter, she does not look English at all. The reason is not hard to find. Hogarth was English; Van Dyke was not.

To Van Dyke the English character was exotic, and if a painter wishes to keep to the grand style, he must shun the exotic like the plague. For what we find interesting in a picture is not how exotic the painter found the subject—nor the consequent caricature he made of it. What holds our interest is how exotic we ourselves find the painter to be, who has made us see through his own strange eyes the unexpected strangeness of the most ordinary things in the world. The exotic as subject is a too easy strangeness which a painter in the grand style must avoid. And national character, to a painter of another country, is the most exotic thing there is.

To a native, his own country may be irritating or idyllic; it is never strange. It is simply a collection of different people, each one with a different life and different ambitions. They have no visible nationality. They are in no way exotic. He feels at home with them because he knows in advance and without too much trouble what they will do next. But for a foreigner, looking at the same people from the outside, their mutual differences are less easy to see. He is aware, instead, of the traits they possess in common, and it is evident to him that the country has a general coloration and a moral climate all its own. This national character that the foreigner perceives, however, is not based on how any one person or set of people actually looks or behaves. It is composed, instead, of that part of the natives' looks and behavior that they think of as generally suitable and unlikely to attract attention, and which the foreigner notices only when these conventions differ sharply from his own.

A preposterous guide to this outside view of national character can be found in the nation's fashion magazines. The kind of people who read a particular magazine can usually be inferred from the products its pages offer for sale. The back sections of adventure magazines are full of reducing belts, exercise charts, false teeth, electric vibrators, hair restorers, trusses, and other appurtenances of the middle-aged. Magazines of literary criticism frequently provide a column for the meeting of lonely hearts; the literary life is perhaps more solitary than we painters imagine. The products advertised in the fashion magazines are beauty, decorum, and how to obtain them. The models who display these garments and lotions are carefully chosen to conform to the ideals of beauty and decorum admired and considered appropriate by the people to whom these products are to be sold. Consequently the fashion plates and photographs of a magazine of women's wear will always exhibit the kind of beauty the women of that nation consider desirable and at the same time normal—in other words, the ideal exterior aspect of their national character.

So that if we are to believe the fashion magazines, the English upper-class woman of today is intellectually incurious, not virginal, but in the technical sense, frigid. The French woman can receive pleasure without vulgarity, and please without cloying. The American woman is an inviolable and self-sufficient citadel, a monster of dandyism. And we are led to infer that success in England is measured by the people one's position can dominate and snub; in France by the people one's intelligence can interest and hold; and in America by the number of people one's charm can attract and keep at bay. Formulas such as these are of course absurd. They are too simple to be true. Even more absurd are the conventions of national character commonly attributed by one nation to another. The qualification of strong and silent for the English, emotional for the Italians, pleasure-loving for the French, and business-like for the Americans, may once have had some small justification in fact; they are today, as much as any such generalization can be, the exact opposite of the truth. One is always finding the English talkative, the Italians logical, the French moral, and the Americans fantastical idealists. But these, too, are incomplete generalizations. National character, except for the purpose of caricature, cannot be described in any such limited terms.

Yet national character does exist, and is unmistakable. It is not the simple tag or packaging Hollywood pretends when it uses Viennese actors for French parts in pictures about Paris—on the grounds, I suppose, that all Europe is equally foreign and speaks with an accent. Such actors can carry conviction only for those spectators who have never encountered a real Parisian or a Viennese. For national character is not made up only of the traits that everyone of a nation has, such as being blond or speaking French, or any series of things everyone in a nation does, like chewing gum or drinking tea. It is also composed of all the things that everyone in the nation thinks it proper not to admit doing. So that it is impossible for anyone who knows Paris or Vienna ever to confuse a Parisian and a Viennese, because the qualities of character and appearance required for living unremarked in Paris and Vienna are not at all the same. These different requirements color every action, every gesture and every elegance of the inhabitants of two cities in an unmistakable way.

National character is something a painter must find a way to deal with. It is an integral part of his sitter's resemblance. A native painter can sense it without effort, and will paint his sitter's national character without ever knowing he has done so. But a foreign painter in a strange land will have a difficult choice to make. To him this national character is exotic. Either he must abandon the grand style for the picturesque, paint the qualities of the sitter that he finds the most striking because they are the most different from his own, and produce a caricature of nationality, as did Sargent and Manet in their Spanish dancers and bull fighters, and Delacroix and David with their Algerians and antique Romans. Or else, if he is to keep in the grand style, he must ignore his sitter's exotic coloration and paint him, not as a foreigner, but as a member of the painter's own nation.

English painting is full of this. Because—and it is a thing we all know and never remember—except for some almost anonymous Elizabethans and a few obscure imitators of Van Dyke, before Hogarth, not one of the well-known English painters was English. Holbein was Swiss, Van Somer, Van Ceulen, and Lely were Dutch, Kneller was German, and Van Dyke himself was Flemish. The English character these imported painters had to paint was, of course, nothing at all like the English character as we think of it today. The English under the Tudors must have been especially different. Foreign visitors to England in the sixteenth century described the English natives in the same terms Victorian travelers used to describe the natives of Italy. They speak of an emotional, musical, mercurial race, frivolous, fond of singing and dancing, generous, quarrelsome, ready to embrace in one minute and draw knives the next, the women of an unrestrained licentiousness—a country of intrigue and double-dealing, where no business, public or private, could be accomplished without a bribe. It is not at all unlike the English character—and for that matter the human character—that Shakespeare describes.

These must have been the people Holbein painted. But this is not the character with which they appear in his pictures, nor would he have been able to give them this character even had he wished. For Holbein was Swiss. To keep his pictures in the grand style he was obliged to ignore his sitter's picturesque foreignness and paint them like himself. Besides, a foreign-born painter cannot but believe that the traits of character admired by his own nation are the ideals of appearance and behavior of all the human race. So that Holbein was very likely trying to flatter these English princes by attributing to them what he would naturally enough consider the noblest of all human qualities—the solid moral dependability of a Basle banker. For the same reasons the English painted by Peter Lely, who was Dutch, look Dutch, and the English portraits of Van Dyke, who was Flemish, look like the rest of the Spanish-Flemish international set who were his usual clients. These gentle and dignified women, these sly and foppish men of the Van Dyke portraits—though they are in all probability what the English under the Stuarts aspired to resemble—have very little in their appearance that is characteristically English. Most certainly they are like no Englishman anybody painted in the eighteenth century. The English in the eighteenth century portraits are convincing as English characters. The painters who painted these Georgian sitters were Englishmen themselves.

Although there had been no English painting before Hogarth, there was no lack of painting tradition on the continent. Hogarth, the first of the English painters, went to the Dutch for his style and instruction. His position as the first native English painter gave him an enviable independence. He had no anterior local tradition of taste to obey, nor was he impressed or influenced by the French taste which was then beginning to come into fashion. This was the taste of the extravagant and licentious regency that preceded the reign of Louis XV in France, and Hogarth as a moralist and as a patriotic Englishman was actively hostile to it. In fact, his best-known pictures, the series of *The Rake's Progress* and of the *Marriage à la Mode*, were painted precisely to deride the English affection of this imported luxury. Consequently, with a sound tradition of technique to work in and with no local or imposed taste to limit his vision—and being a man of considerable genius as well—Hogarth was able to explore the singularities of his sitters' appearance with a freedom no subsequent English painter was ever again permitted to exercise. These people he painted are unmistakably English. They differ in no respect from the English described by writers as far apart as Aubrey and Defoe. They are people one could know and be entertained by knowing, and his pictures depict them with all the salt and peculiarities they undoubtedly possessed. Hogarth is unquestionably the greatest of the English painters. His work has freshness, genius, wit. But it is in the grand, not in the noble style. There is no elegance in it, nothing to impress the French. By 1750, by the time there were enough painters, with Reynolds and Gainsborough, to form a recognizable English school, the French and their taste could no longer be disregarded.

Already by the beginning of the century the French taste had begun to influence the English. The easiest example is perhaps to be found in the poets. Take these pastorals—of Dryden, who wrote, before the French taste, for Purcell's music:

> Fairest isle, all isles excelling,
> Seat of pleasures and of loves,
> Venus here will choose her dwelling,
> And forsake her Cyprian groves.

And of Pope, who helped to introduce the French taste, or at any rate, the French correction, into English:

> O'er golden sands let rich Pactolus flow,
> And trees weep amber on the banks of Po;
> Bless Thames's shores the brightest beauties yield.
> Feed here my lambs, I'll seek no distant field.

Both have the same subject—love in England. But one is fun, the other an astonishing contrivance. More than this, the florid and skillful artificiality of Pope's youthful poem is in the exact style of the French taste of the time at which it was composed, of the regency before Louis XV. A few years later, Hogarth was ridiculing the English aping of the same French fashions. By the middle of the century, the French taste, this time the more restrained taste of the court of Louis XV, had come to dominate English manners just as it had come to dominate the manners of the rest of Europe; and the English national character—at least among the upper classes—changed to conform to this new internationalism.

This change is reflected in the portraits. There is as much difference between Gainsborough's and Hogarth's sitters as there had been between Hogarth's and Van Dyke's. Hogarth's subjects had been a country-bred aristocracy; Gainsborough's were the bon ton of a town. Unlike Hogarth's sitters, the people Gainsborough painted never seem in any way eccentric. At most they are only affected. The men, as they appear in the pictures, are strong, not flighty or artistic (though many of Gainsborough's clients, to show perhaps that they have accomplished the Grand Tour, exhibit an air of Frenchified ambiguity), kindly, for the most part, and competent, but without intellectual or religious passions, and governed by social conventions rather than by any inner compulsions. The women, to quote Pope again, have no character at all—silly, pretty, subject to the vapors, demanding flattery (the more outrageously false, the more acceptable, was Chesterfield's opinion), of more energy and assurance than intellectual distinction, and—if the number of children's portraits they caused to be painted is any evidence—running their households with an iron hand.

These sitters put a new problem to the painters: how

to depict them with all the charm, urbanity and nobility their French-formed tastes demanded. For this purpose the straightforward, middle-class, burgher painting style that Hogarth had adopted from the Dutch was not enough. Further elegance and grandeurs were required. So Gainsborough went to Van Dyke and to the painters of the French court to learn elegance (to France only in spirit, however; actually to London where he studied with a French painter and engraver named Gravelot). But Reynolds went, in the flesh, to Italy—to Raphael, the Carracci, and Giulio Romano, for the noble style. He returned to England with the material for his celebrated *Discourses*.

Reynolds's *Discourses* are perhaps the best known, the least read, and, I believe, the least readable of all books on painting in English. They were commencement addresses to the painting students of the Royal Academy, of which Reynolds was first president. So pompous and Ciceronian that they might have been, and probably were, by Dr. Johnson himself, they praise the Italian Eclectics (Guido Reni, the Carracci, and the others who thought to produce great pictures by the simple expedient of taking from each of the greatest painters—in their opinion Michelangelo, Raphael and Leonardo—his greatest quality, and then combining them); and they advocate a nobility of line and a simplicity of color that Reynolds himself never even attempted to adopt—much to the annoyance of poor William Blake.

Blake is an extremely interesting moral and mystical writer and an excellent poet. But as a painter he is only a minor illustrator in the ornamental style, and a follower of the Swiss-born painter Henry Fuseli. Fuseli's contribution to English painting was an adaptation of the Italian Mannerists—the followers of Michelangelo, Leonardo and Raphael—to the Greek Revival style. Perhaps the most familiar example of the Greek Revival in painting is David's unfinished portrait of Madame Récamier. The lady in the picture reclines on a chaise-longue beside a standing lamp—both pieces of furniture taken from Percier's and Fontaine's recent reconstructions of the decorative styles of Pompeii—dressed in a transparent and clinging garment, almost a nightgown, her pretty feet bare. All this, to us so charmingly Directoire, was to David and his public authentically Greek. To Blake and to his time, the Greek Revival was the advanced in taste, even, in the political sense of the word, the revolutionary. I can only suppose that it is this titillating and incompatible mixture in Blake's work—of English stained glass, Gothic Revival, Michelangelo, the Ideal Nude and Directoire—that has maintained, at least in the literary world, Blake's undeserved reputation as a painter.

But Blake was a poet and believed that words should have some real connection with the things they are used to describe. He was outraged to find that Reynolds's rhetoric had no relation to Reynolds's painting. He expressed voluminously on the margins of a copy of the *Discourses* his exasperation with Reynolds's painting and his endorsement of Reynolds's principles. Reynolds, not being a literary man and not really believing in the meaning of the words he used, disregarded his own principles and painted well and easily. Blake followed Reynolds's principles exactly and landed in a morass of singularity, limitation and mannerism. In fact, he landed not in painting at all, but squarely in the arts and crafts.

The precepts in Reynolds's *Discourses* define the noble style. They are about simplicity of color—using simple reds, yellows, blues and greens—about nobility of line and of gesture, about the importance of generalized, or ideal beauty, where the painter is required to remove a squint or straighten a model's nose for the better elucidation of a moral principle.

When Reynolds himself followed the noble style his *Discourses* advocate, he did it as badly as anyone else. His excursions into allegory are few, timid and unconvincing. *Mrs. Siddons as the Tragic Muse* is still an actress, and the *The Graces decorating Hymen* is more earnest than inspired. His portraits, on the other hand, are pictures of real people. Perhaps that is what Reynolds really meant in his *Discourses*—how to put the noble style to work to give his sitters human dignity. He, at any rate, is the only one of his contemporaries who succeeded. Gainsborough lent his sitters a feline sophistication straight out of Versailles, an air of society, snobbery and visiting lists; Romney the *haut ton* of a fashion magazine; and Raeburn and Lawrence the well-washed appearance of the man in the advertisement who has just bought a car. Gainsborough is far more brilliant than Reynolds, Copley more accomplished, and Hogarth in every way more interesting. Even Reynolds's technique is said to be faulty by everyone from William Blake, who boasted (to the tune of "Yankee Doodle") of its impermanence (*When Sr Joshua Reynolds died/All Nature was degraded;/The King drop'd a tear in the*

Queen's Ear/And all his Pictures Faded.), to present-day restorers who complain that Reynolds's repeated glazes, scumbles, retouchings, and intemperate experimentation with painting media render his pictures exceedingly difficult to clean. Nor is there any apparent influence on Reynolds's painting of Raphael, Guido Reni or the noble style. The noble style was an official fashion of the time greatly admired by the poets and writers, just as is the abstract style today. It was enough that Reynolds could write in its praise and was not obliged as well to add to the acres of dreary and theatrical painting that the noble style engendered—Benjamin West's *Death of Wolfe*, for example, with its absurdities of Italianate grandeurs, suavities and gestures, applied to red Indians, a British general and a Canadian scene. But if Reynolds's painting has little of the noble style, there is something in it of the grand style, a sort of honest straightforwardness, a simplicity and a human directness that is rare in this century of French taste.

Perhaps it was Reynolds's visit to Italy—where there are more sorts of painting than the literary fashions of his day admired—which permitted him to by-pass the French taste and paint his people real. The Spaniard Goya and the American John Singleton Copley also managed to avoid the French taste, but by quite another method. It was, I think, by being provincials and consequently not knowing any better.

Spain and America in the eighteenth century were difficult countries to get to—Spain even more than America—and in such provinces away from the French court, the refinements of the French taste were either exaggerated or ignored. Even as near as Italy, the ladies permitted themselves extravagances of costume forbidden at Versailles, where the height of the headdress and the width of the panniers were regulated by royal protocol. In countries difficult to reach, fashionable taste was hard to know. Clients for portraits in such places would be unlikely to share the standard European notions of proper appearance, or to understand the details of which this elegance was composed. A competent painter is always rare in the provinces. His very rarity gives him authority, and his clients, who have no better guide, will probably accept without demur his version of their souls. A painter, left to himself, always prefers to paint his sitter as he sees him, rather than as an example of some ideal of virtue or decorum. So that portraits painted in the provinces, even at the height of the influence of the French taste, often came out as pictures of interesting human beings.

These provincial portraits, however, are likely to be overelaborate in their painting. In the great centers, where there is much painting and many painters, there develops a general vocabulary of painting which the public understands and accepts. A painter does not have to do everything in each picture in order to prove his ability. He can permit himself short cuts, suggest details he does not paint, and still be understood. But in the provinces, where not much painting is made or seen, and to a provincial public that does not have the habit of looking at pictures, the painter knows that everything in a picture must be explained. So that the mark of the provincial painter is overscrupulousness and excessive detail. The excessive detail and finish of the English pre-Raphaelite painters, and the immediate popularity of their pictures on this account, is the direct result of the provincial situation of both British painting and the British public in the middle of the nineteenth century. The same thing can be said of the late Grant Wood in the American scene.

Copley was just such a provincial painter. His painting style was formed in America, where there were few painters. Later he went to live in England, where there were many. There he broadened his style and got rid of his provincial stiffness and unnecessary detail. But this attitude toward his sitters, formed away from the influence of the French court, he did not change. And although he traveled all the way from being a naïve painter to becoming one of the most skillful and elaborate of the portraitists of his day, he never abandoned his original and provincial disdain for the fashionable amenities of appearance. Consequently the people in Copley's pictures remain to this day real, alive and interesting.

Goya's painting, on the contrary, was never naïve. Goya had studied in Italy. And if the Spain of Goya's time was provincial, Spanish painting was not. The full force of the French taste, nevertheless, could not cross the Pyrenees. The peasants of Goya's early pictures engage in the rural occupations so admired at Versailles, such as dairy farming and sheep herding. But even the extreme fashionableness of these pursuits cannot make Goya's milkmaids and shepherdesses any different from what Goya saw them to be, the native Spaniards of his native Spain. In fact, I think it can be said that our whole idea of Spain comes from what Goya saw and painted. It is Goya we see in the costumes and ceremonies of the bull ring. And Carmen was born from the dark glances of the Duchess of Alba, dressed by Goya as a woman of Madrid.

These people, in Hogarth, in Reynolds, in Goya, in Copley, are real. And this is the grand style. For the grand style is not a style at all. It is not a way of painting. It is only the painter's greatest subject. It is what every painter strives to paint. It is the painter's view of ultimate reality.

CHAPTER FOUR

THE PLANNED PICTURE

> LADY BASSET (opening the album and turning a page or two): Real Art. My passion!
>
> Henry James, *The Album*

Painting as it is practiced today, the painting of our own time, the most conservative as well as the most modern, is the result of two profound revolutions in technique each of which took roughly a hundred years. Because of the first of these revolutions our pictures are in oil; because of the second, they are systematic improvisations. It is the direct consequence of these two revolutions that a picture by a living painter, say by Matisse, resembles, for instance, a Filippino Lippi in no way at all, except in the two painters' undisputed ability.

The first of these revolutions began somewhere around 1400 with the discovery, attributed to Van Eyck, of a practical method of painting in oil, and ended with the complete mastery of oil paint by the Venetians a hundred years later. It freed the painter from his dependence on outline and gave him an ease and speed in painting and a variety of effects undreamed of before. It also enabled him to paint on canvas, so that he could paint pictures as large as he wished and which were no longer necessarily fixed to the walls for which they were originally designed.

The second revolution is less precisely dated. It began somewhere in the middle of the eighteenth century with the discovery by Fragonard, Guardi, and others of the charm of the sketch and the delights of improvisation. It was completed late in the nineteenth century by the Impressionists whose pictures were methodically improvised. It freed the painter from the restrictions of the planned picture which had by now become a burden. This second revolution has been so complete that few people today, not even many painters, can think of the act of painting as anything except improvisation. Yet almost every picture made before the middle of the nineteenth century was a planned picture, painted with the help of drawings, and generally on top of a composition worked out on the canvas beforehand in monochrome. Such a proceeding is ancient and respectable. It was precisely this firm basis of the planned picture, complemented by the fluid ease Van Eyck's new oil paint allowed, which made possible the brilliance, rapidity, and freedom of the great Venetians.

What we ourselves are accustomed to think of as oil painting—painting, in fact, as it is practiced today—stems directly from these Venetians. Our painting has little to do with the tempera tradition of which Van Eyck's way of painting still forms a part. Our painting is in the freer tradition established by the great painters of Venice. This tradition differs radically from all the fresco and tempera tradition that preceded it in that it has none of tempera's linear rigidity. Here, as is always the case, the materials the painter has to use dictate the style of his painting, and tempera is rigid by nature. The painter in tempera has great difficulty correcting his mistakes and masking his changes. His picture must begin and must remain clean, precise, and neat. He begins with outline; his composition must remain linear.

Colors in tempera, and in fresco, do not have the same tone wet and dry. They dry lighter, and in an unpredictable way. Once they are dry, they are difficult, almost impossible, to match with a fresh mixture of wet paint. The painter is obliged to mix up in advance every tone of all the colors he is to use in the picture he is working on. He must keep all these paint mixtures around him wet in little pots until the picture is finished—no matter how foul they begin to smell, which is soon enough, for there is generally some egg or glue in the concoction. Large simple areas, like backgrounds with uniform shading from light to dark, require extreme virtuosity to execute. In fact, any gradation of color at all is troublesome. The paint dries too rapidly to blend. Transitions of tone must be achieved by cross-hatching. Any change of plan involves much labor. The painter must know in advance, and in detail, what he intends to do. He begins with the outline and fills it in. Once the outline is established, it can be changed only with greatest difficulty.

The oil painter, on the other hand, can change and correct at will. His paint remains comfortably wet. He can obtain the most subtle gradations with ease. All he needs is to smear. His picture can be endlessly repainted.

To match tones is easy. His colors are the same whether wet or dry. He has no reason to be neat. He can begin by painting as crudely as he pleases, in great rough areas of light and dark, and then refine and adjust them later. An outline fixed at the beginning would be only a hindrance. He can put it in as a detail at the end, or even, if he wishes, leave it out altogether. He can permit himself the most outrageous freedoms and the most monumental messes. Just as the art of the tempera painter is concerned with lines and the areas of color the lines contain, the oil painter's technique has first of all to do with light-and-dark in tone and back-and-forth in space.

The Venetians were the first to exploit the range of freedom the new oil paint allowed. At any rate, oil is what Vasari and his contemporaries called the Van Eyck painting medium. But it was like no oil paint that anybody knows about today, or has known about for the last three hundred years. It was a paint which allowed the painter to paint microscopic detail, a thing no oil paint we have today will do. And unlike any of the temperas or water-thinned mediums we know about, it evidently kept the same tone wet and dry. It also permitted the painter to achieve minute differences between black and almost black such as can be obtained in no medium, so far as I know, that anybody has ever heard of—either egg, oil, water color, glue, wax, milk, varnish, or any of their combinations. These small accurate differences in the dark tones could be obtained perhaps with pigment ground in some heavy, honey-like varnish. But with such a heavy, sticky vehicle, fine detail is impossible. It has been claimed recently that

Van Eyck had spirits of turpentine, distilled by the alchemists, for thinning his colors and getting his fine detail. But this would explain nothing. Spirits of turpentine is a great convenience to the oil painter for keeping his brushes clean while he works. But if enough turpentine is used to thin a heavy varnish paint for fine detail, the advantages of the varnish are lost and the paint dries flat and paler. Any change in the tone of the paint would keep the painter from obtaining the close-valued blacks and the sharp detail in the deepest shadows that these early oil paintings all possess.

There is an unfinished Van Eyck in Antwerp—of the building of a cathedral and St. Barbara seated in front of it—which shows the steps by which the painting was done. The picture was first drawn in on the white ground of a plaster-covered wooden panel, and carefully shaded in brown water color or ink. The drawing is minute, complete and detailed, exactly as if the rest of the picture were to be done in tempera. This drawing was then colored with layers of the oil paint. As one can see, the construction is in no way different from the usual tempera picture, except for the mysterious smoothness and richness characteristic of the Van Eyck medium itself.

The mysterious Van Eyck medium is, in fact, one of the most celebrated of the lost secrets of the old masters, and its rediscovery is constantly being claimed. But whether one of these inventions is indeed the Van Eyck secret actually is of little importance to the painter of today. For however much a contemporary painter may admire the Van Eyck effects, he admires them as an archaeologist rather than as an emulator. The limitations the Van Eyck painting methods would impose on his own work he would find burdensome and artificial.

The Van Eyck secret, whatever it may have been, furnished the early Flemish painters with rich tones and easy gradations which tempera could not provide. Brought into Italy, the Van Eyck oil-painting method lost some of its original character and stiffness. Even painters like Raphael and Leonardo used their oil paint as if it were only a richer way of painting tempera pictures. But in the hands of the Venetians, oil painting turned into something quite different from any other sort of painting that had ever been done before. It lost every tempera characteristic and became a large, free, loose and easy way to work, not unlike the free and easy way of painting which oil provides today. But oil painting and the tempera painting it replaced still had this in common: all pictures in both techniques, from Cimabue until after Ingres, were elaborately underpainted and planned in advance. By a division of labor both logical and simple, first they were drawn; then they were colored. If one is to believe Cennino Cennini, who described the early tempera methods, Cimabue made his plan in brown and white and green, and in tempera. Ingres made his in black and white, and in oil. It was not until the Impressionists and their revolution that a respectable picture could be made with no plan at all.

Venetian pictures were not improvised. They were planned in advance. They began with drawings. These drawings were not exercises in skill. They were the plans made by the painter for his work. That is why so many of the old masters' drawings still exist; they made so many. It was from these drawings, and not from nature or the living model, that the composition of the picture was arranged, and the picture itself, if it was to be a large one, was sketched in on the canvas. Next the underpainting, the chiaroscuro, the light-and-dark of the picture, was laid in, painted in a scale of neutral browns or grays, in water color, or a tempera emulsion, or in some oil medium so doctored that it would dry at once. Even the underpainting was sometimes executed from drawings, without the presence of the model. This underpainting was the structural framework of the picture. It was nowhere finished in detail. It had no color. It was in pale tones and without accents. But when it was complete every principal feature of the picture was supposed to be in place, ready for color and finishing. On top of this the color itself was applied, in "scumbles" and in "glazes." "Glazes" are darker coats of more or less transparent paint, and "scumbles" are light rubbings of a paler, opaque paint which—by the same optical effect that makes a mountain seem bluer on a hazy day—make cooler and somewhat paler the tones on which they are applied.

As one can see, such a process is no more an improvisation than is the tailoring of a suit of clothes. It is a process of manufacture. It is, in fact, so much a process of manufacture that the great Venetians, Tintoretto in particular, and perhaps most of all the Fleming Peter Paul Rubens, can scarcely be called painters at all. They are instead producers, directors of factories, turning out their pictures by the same methods of employing, grouping and subordinating men of specialized talent, which are used for turning out pictures in Hollywood today. The Disney Studios are an even more exact comparison.

Like all manufacturers, the old masters had their secrets. The precise details of how their pictures were made is by no means clear. It is quite easy to find out how some of the eighteenth century pictures were painted. There are manuals of instruction written by painters for painting students, explaining how it was to be done, which are still easy enough to follow. But it is extremely difficult to know exactly what series of mediums and recipes of cookery the older painters employed. Organic chemistry has no method of analysis subtle enough to determine the composition of a varnish or a medium in one of these pictures when we do not have the formula. Even when we have the recipes written down, we cannot be certain the names used for the ingredients have still the same meaning today. Amber varnish, for instance, occurring so frequently in these recipes, is most likely not amber at all, but was made with some other resin which looked like it. Such recipes, moreover, depend for their success as much on tricks of hand and temperature as does the mixing of mayonnaise or the making of bread. And it is highly unlikely, besides, that any two painters followed the same recipes or processes.

Most mysterious of all in this mysterious field is the painting of Jan Vermeer. His paint surface has a quality unlike any other. How it was achieved, nobody understands. Other masters are less difficult to copy. There are pictures which simulate so well the appearance of a Titian or a Rembrandt, that their falsity can be proved only by documents. There are certainly many pictures wrongly attributed to these masters and to others which no one questions because of the irreproachable quality of their paint. But the paint quality of a Vermeer, no one, as far as I know, except the notorious Dutch forger Van Meegeren, has ever been able to imitate. Van Meegeren, however, imitated it so well that he was able to sell his pictures to the German high command as undoubted originals, and his forgeries were sponsored by reputable museums and reproduced as originals in text books.

The Vermeer surface itself is like little else in painting. It is a sort of eggshell lacquer. But Vermeer's unrivaled achievement is the air that fills his pictures. His paintings seem aquariums of air. The objects in them bathe in this real fluid. This astonishing effect is chiefly due to Vermeer's mastery of the most difficult of all the technical problems of painting—the problem of the edges.

Edges are where any two tones or colors in a picture come together. They must always be handled with care. All the Venetian or post-Venetian painters, for example, are careful to fuzz and render imprecise the edge which separates a light area from a dark. If one examines the outline of a cheek in any sixteenth, seventeenth or eighteenth century portrait which has a dark background, he will find that the light tone does not stop with a hard line. Instead, the light of the face leaks over into the dark of the background, and the gradation will be anywhere from a sixteenth to a quarter of an inch in width or even wider, depending on the distance from which the painter meant the picture to be viewed. This spreading of the light confuses the eye, gives the illusion of the presence of light and air, and serves to situate the painted objects well within the space behind the surface of the canvas.

The effective varying and blending of the edges is difficult to accomplish in direct painting—that is to say in painting where each tone is put down as it is to appear in the finished picture—and requires considerable attention on the painter's part, no matter in which way he paints. In fact it is an axiom of the schools that a painter who can paint edges can paint anything. And neglect of the problem of the edges accounts for much of the brutality and harshness we complain of in the virtuoso painting of our own time, from Boldini to Howard Chandler Christy and Augustus John.

Of this problem Vermeer is the supreme master. All his edges, not only the boundaries between light and dark, but all edges without exception, are fused. Small isolated spots of color, such as one can see in the little picture in the National Gallery of a girl wearing a sort of Chinese hat, spread out and melt along their borders like tiny flecks of sunlight. This careful, skillful blending of the edges is why air seems to penetrate these pictures and why their colors seem to reach our eyes from deep within a block of palpable and yet transparent jelly.

In addition, the surface of Vermeer's pictures is singularly unified. The entire picture seems to have been painted with the same size brush, without undue efforts on the painter's part, and keeping well within the limits of an easy skill, almost as if the picture had been executed by some mechanical or photographic means. No passage seems more worked on than another. The painter appears to have found them all equally simple to do, which give these pictures that equalized tension we today find so attractive.

The oddest thing about the Vermeer pictures is that Vermeer—unless he himself intended to deceive us—painted directly with no underpainting at all. In the famous

Painter and His Model in the Habsburg Collection, the painter is shown beginning his picture on a clean gray canvas marked only with a few lines in white chalk; he proceeds by painting, in color and in detail, the blue plumes on his model's head dress. This is extraordinary. The picture is being painted without underpainting and in proper color. Most extraordinary of all, it is being painted piecemeal. The plumes are being finished first. The background will then, presumably, be painted up to them. This is not the way an experienced painter sets out to paint his edges—then or today. But incredible or not, this seems to have been the way that Vermeer worked.

However little we may know about Vermeer's painting methods, the forger Van Meegeren must have been able to reproduce something of the quality of the Vermeer surface. Now that the forgeries have been exposed, it is difficult to see how Van Meegeren's pictures could have deceived anyone. Their literary sentiment has nothing of Vermeer's reticence or distinction. It is instead on the emotional level of the devotional pictures of the nineteenth century Munich painter Hofmann and the sentimental Sunday school cards that they inspired. I have not seen the forgeries themselves. I have seen only their photographs. I cannot be certain what their surface is like. But these forgeries could not have been taken seriously by anybody, unless they had possessed something of the characteristic surface and paint qualities of the real Vermeers.

Van Meegeren's painting method, however, was one that Vermeer himself could not have followed. According to Dr. P. Coremans, who made a laboratory examination of the forged pictures and published an account of them, it was a very curious method indeed. Van Meegeren began by using as a base for his pictures some worthless seventeenth century paintings on canvas. He cleaned the paint off the canvas with paint remover, leaving, however, as much as he could of the original priming with its characteristic crackle which age alone can give. On this canvas he painted his picture using only the pigment available to Vermeer—including real ultramarine blue made from powdered lapis lazuli—the pigments made into paint by being ground in one of the new synthetic resins dissolved in a volatile solvent; these of course did not exist in Vermeer's time. Van Meegeren must have had some trick of handling or some particular solvent which Dr. Coremans does not disclose. Ordinarily, such a resin paint is difficult to work with. It dries by evaporation of the solvent and not, as does oil paint, by chemical changes in the binding medium itself. Fresh coats put on with a brush are likely to pick up the dry coats underneath.

Whatever the trick may have been, when the painting was finished, the picture was put in a slow oven and baked. The heat hardened the resin binder, and the paint became as resistant to the solvents restorers use for cleaning pictures as if it had been painted for hundreds of years. This is important in a forgery, for it is principally by the paint's resistance to a solvent that a restorer can determine a picture's age. The painting was then varnished. It was pulled around a roller to produce a crackle, if possible a continuation of the crackle in the priming of the seventeenth century canvas underneath. The crackle was dirtied with ink so that it would be more visible. The whole was thereupon varnished with an orange varnish to give the picture a golden tone appropriate to its artificial age.

A spectroscopic analysis of the blue pigment in the pictures furnished one of the proofs of fraud. Among the spectrum lines characteristic of ultramarine blue—the lines of sulphur, silicon, aluminum and so on—the spectroscope also showed the lines that cobalt gives. Van Meegeren had been betrayed by his color merchant. The real ultramarine Van Meegeren was sold (extremely expensive, worth, I am told, its weight in solid gold) had been adulterated with the cheaper cobalt blue, which was not known until some one hundred and fifty years after Vermeer's death.

The most striking thing, however, about Van Meegeren's process is the baking of the product. Is it possible that it was this very baking process which produced for Van Meegeren the characteristic Vermeer quality? Could it have been that Vermeer himself painted in some soft varnish medium, and subjected the finished picture to a cooking process such as this, which softened his paint, caused it to run slightly (as sometimes happens when painted china is fired) and in this unorthodox way produced the even surface and fusion of edges which made his pictures so different from all others? Strange as this conjecture may seem, and improbable as I believe it to be, it is not entirely impossible. We know as little about some of the sixteenth and seventeenth century painting methods as we do about the Van Eyck secret, or for that matter, about the methods of the masters of the tempera painting which preceded it.

There is no such mystery, however, about the technical methods of the late eighteenth and early nineteenth century painters. These are fully explained in painting manuals of the time, some of them written by the painters themselves. Let us look at one of these pictures to see how it was done.

In the Frick Collection hangs a portrait by Reynolds of General John Burgoyne. The Frick, half museum, half habitable palace, redolent of potted ferns and private string quartets, is exactly, I am sure, what James's Mr. Verver of *The Golden Bowl* was planning to build in American City for Charlotte and his treasures. This portrait of our celebrated enemy is precisely the one English portrait Mr. Verver's sense of fitness and oddity would have chosen for an American collection. The General is a handsome man with a red coat and a roving eye. His waistcoat is gray, his breeches are gray, and his left hand, half in his pocket, is gray also. The hand is not gloved. It is simply incomplete. Reynolds, for some reason or other, perhaps because of the obvious energy and impatience of his military sitter, never got his picture finished.

These unfinished pictures are not as uncommon as one might suppose. There is another in the same museum, a portrait painted by Goya some sixty years later of a Doña Maria Martinez de Puga, which also has a gray hand. The sitter is holding her fan in what appears to be a clumsy gray mitt, which some ingenious restorer, or perhaps even Goya himself, has tried to excuse by drawing on its back the three white lines that would indicate the ribs of a glove. But even as a glove, the hand is not convincing. It is much too rough. This is how Goya began a picture. It is not like this that he would have called it finished.

The gray hands on both pictures are only the uncovered portions of an underpainting with which these painters began their pictures and which was called, with considerable reason, "the dead painting." Their method was not too different from the Venetians'. The painter began with a warm-toned canvas and laid out his picture in oil paint, using as colors only black and white tempered with just enough of some warm earth color, some red or yellow clay, to kill the unpleasant steely violet-blue that the straight mixture of black and white produces. The painting manuals of the time give various recipes for this "dead color," but its use was quite general. In a book written by Thomas Sully (all painters, I am sure, write books) Reynolds himself is reported to have "preferred using for a portrait only white, yellow, vermilion, and black in the flesh." The vermilion, and perhaps the yellow, I assume from other manuals were reserved for the second stage of painting. The panels of the Fragonard room in the Frick Collection—these incredibly elegant and gentle panels where Louis XV and Madame de Pompadour are pictured as children playing at love—were begun, as one can see, with white and burnt sienna, a red-orange rust color, a great deal of which has been left uncovered. Ingres and, I believe, most of the other nineteenth century "Classicists" used only black and white. At any rate that is the way Ingres's unfinished *Odalisque* was left, a sad, gray monochrome.

There was no set rule as to how finished and detailed the "dead painting" was to be. The result aimed at was a loose, free, but quite complete picture with everything in its place and all the canvas covered, in a warm monochrome or in a pearly gray. According to Sully this "dead painting" was done without the sitter, from drawings made beforehand. When the "dead painting" was dry, the sitter was called in and the picture was completely repainted in the proper colors of the sitter's clothes and complexion. This next coat of paint was not a thin glaze. It was quite as thick as the "dead painting" itself although some of the gray underpaint was allowed to show through where bluish shadows were needed in the face or hands or elsewhere: the gray left uncovered or partly covered looks a great deal bluer than one would imagine offhand. Then warm, even vermilion, accents were painted in the folds of the flesh, between the fingers, and in the ears and nostrils. Though it was not considered quite proper to improve the sitter's features (the character, according to Gilbert Stuart, residing in the nose), nevertheless there was nothing reprehensible in attributing to him a livelier coloring than he actually possessed. On top of this, particularly in Romantic times, a brown or orange varnish—"soup," it was called—was sometimes applied to give the picture the mellow tones of age.

The battlefields, porticos, columns, groves or simple trees that form the backgrounds of these pictures were part of the furniture of the painter's studio. They were painted on muslin, exactly like the photographer's backgrounds of our childhood, and when needed unfurled behind the sitter to provide him with a setting appropriate to his tastes or circumstances—a villa, a vista or a cloud. Thus the painter could avoid the difficult problem of painting with an equal precision the real and the imagined.

This is roughly the method Reynolds used to paint General Burgoyne. Goya's lady with her fan is less complete. Unless she has suffered a thorough skinning by some unskillful restorer, which is hardly likely, there is here only the "dead color" with at the most an hour's work on top of it—the background painted tan and the face brushed in lightly in pink. Most of Goya's portraits, in fact, look as if they had been executed very rapidly and probably in three sittings: one for a "dead painting" of the sketchiest description, in warm black and gray on a canvas painted in advance a brick red; one for the flesh tones and the local color of the costume; and a third for accents, finishing and corrections. The paint is very thin, and the hot red spots one can see in so many of the Goyas today are the result of overcleaning. It is the brick-red ground showing through the now transparent paint.

In its essentials, all this is the way the Venetians had painted. The recipes and mediums had changed considerably. Some of the colors are not the same. Reynolds and Goya, for example, had the new inexpensive Prussian blue to take the place of Titian's costly ultramarine. The secret of the transparent copper green which Veronese used so successfully has now been lost. But Reynolds and Goya still painted—just as did Titian and Veronese—planned pictures whose composition was first worked out in lights and darks, to which color was then added. The method accounts for the comparative stability of these pictures. A picture constructed on a framework of light and dark, with fairly simple colors superimposed, suffers less from the degeneration of one of these colors than does a picture of the Impressionists or a picture of our own day. Here the composition depends, not on a pattern of values, but on elaborate harmonies and subtle arrangements among the colors themselves. A red fades in a Titian; nothing essential is lost. The picture becomes simply a Titian without red. But if a red fades in a Van Gogh, the whole effect of the picture is distorted.

Simplicity of technique and relative stability were the advantages the planned picture offered. It is then by no means strange that the picture in chiaroscuro, and with color added, remained for almost three hundred years the normal kind of painting. Nor did it disappear from standard practice until long after the perfection of photography; until late in the nineteenth century, when the painter's subject matter had changed and his materials had become portable, when he could set up in the woods and fields his color box and tripod—no more cumbersome by now than Lewis Carroll's camera—and like the camera, and with as little planning, take Nature by surprise.

CHAPTER FIVE

THE BRUSH STROKE AND THE PHOTOGRAPH

> Mr. Ferguson, the self-taught philosopher, told him of a new invented machine which went without horses; a man sat in it and turned a handle, which worked a spring that drove it forward. "Then, Sir, (said Johnson) what is gained is, the man has his choice whether he will move himself alone, or himself and the machine too."
>
> Boswell, *The Life of Samuel Johnson*

In the middle of the nineteenth century the technique of painting changed completely. The eighteenth century had been full of natural philosophy. Franklin, Johnson, Voltaire, Louis XVI—everybody—played with scientific marvels and chemical experiments. The nineteenth century was full of technical inventions. Two of them the painters found particularly interesting. In fact, they were both discovered by painters. Somewhere in the 1830's, the French painter Daguerre (or it may have been his associate with the wonderful name of Nicéphore Niepce) invented photography, and an American painter named Rand invented the collapsible tin tube. Daguerre's invention was bought by the French government and most generously turned over to the public in 1839. Rand's tin tube was adopted by the English color merchants Winsor and Newton in 1841 to contain their paints, and an artists' material catalogue of Dimes and Elan of 1843 offers—along with "India Rubber Prepared Canvas" and "Newly Invented Zinc Tablets"—"oil colors in ordinary bladders or in patent collapsible tin tubes." These two inventions, the tin tube and the photograph, changed the whole character of painting. And 1841, when photography began generally to be practiced, and artists' colors could be bought ready to use in tubes, is the exact date when the change begins.

Before this time, artists' colors had been sold, not as paint already prepared and ready to use, but as powders, gums and lumps, or, at the most, mixed to a stiff paste with spirits of turpentine. It was the painter himself, or his assistant, who made these powders into paint by laboriously grinding them in some suitable medium or drying oil. And this had to be done not too long before they were to be used, otherwise they would dry up. How to make paint was one of the things a painter had to know. The recipes had been handed down for hundreds of years. The traditions were conservative and sound. It was easy to vary the character of the paint to suit the needs of whatever picture the painter had in hand. All he had to do was to vary the composition of the medium in which the pigments were ground. The great variety of mediums which were employed can be judged from the immense variety of textures and surfaces the oil painting of the post-Renaissance tradition displays. Think for example of the extraordinary difference in surface, texture and handling between a Greco and a fruit picture by the Dutch painter Jan de Heem. Yet both were painted in what is loosely called oil.

It cannot be denied that homemade paint had its drawbacks. It did not keep. It had to be made fresh almost every single day, particularly if it was made from one of the faster-drying pigments. Because the paint was too liquid to be carried about on a palette in a color box, homemade paint limited the painter to the painting which could be done at home. Consequently landscapes were painted in the studio from sketches. Cennino Cennini tells his fourteenth century readers how, for the painting of mountains, some clean rocks were to be brought into the studio and the mountains painted from these. This of course was a much earlier time, but the same tradition persisted. It was not until a method had been devised for holding and preserving the too liquid paint that the painter acquired his present habit of going out of doors and placing himself to paint in the midst of nature.

Water-color paints, of course, have always been portable. A pigment ground with gum or mucilage could be soaked up on a rag and dried, or the paint itself dried into a hard cake. When the color was to be used, it could be soaked off the rag in a little water, or rubbed off the cake with a wet brush. No ingenious new invention was needed. From the earliest times painters have had water-color kits that were compact and easy to carry about, and water colors have always been painted out of doors. Indeed the water-color landscapes which Dürer painted from nature somewhere around the beginning of the sixteenth century could be easily mistaken for the work of a German Romantic painter of the 1880's. There is no essential difference in the means employed and in the effect achieved. But no landscape in oil, made before the new portable oil paints, and in the studio, could possibly be mistaken for a picture painted with the new tube colors and out of doors. Constable's little picture and the Roman landscapes of Corot seem to be exceptions to this. But these are small pictures, really sketches, painted, I am sure, from nature and probably with colors contained in the bladders which the color merchants of the early part of the century used for holding paint—impractical and messy as these bladders must have been.

But the new tin tube was portable, clean and economical. Since by the aid of this invention it became easy to paint landscapes from nature, it became equally easy for the painter, at the demand of a new "Realism," to extend the practice and to paint his figure pieces as well directly from the human model—as did Corot and Courbet—without the intervention of any drawing between the painter's first sharp impression of the subject and his finished picture.

The change from painting from sketches in a studio to painting from nature on the spot, enormous as it is, is not the sole reason for the difference one sees in painting after 1841. An even more striking difference comes in a change in the character of the new paint itself.

The new tube was a great improvement on the little bladders the color merchants had been using. But like all modern inventions, the tin tube was far from perfect. As one would expect, it was not completely airtight. Paints made with the same drying oils the painter would himself have used to make his paints at home, dried much too rapidly to suit the distribution methods of a commercial manufacturer. The painter himself would probably have ground his pigments in walnut or linseed oil. But linseed oil becomes gummy in the tube after a certain time, and nut oil (or so I am told—I have never used it) turns rancid. Consequently the color manufacturers began to use the oil made from poppy seed, which dries more slowly, remains sweet in the tube, and does not become gummy or stringy no matter how long the paint remains unsold on the color merchants' shelves. These new colors are responsible for the brittle, rough, impasto paint surface so characteristic of the painting of our time, a surface not to be found in painting before these manufactured colors came into general use.

The paint made by the painter himself with linseed oil generally contains enough pigment to cover well and does not have to be put on thick. But such paint is somewhat fluid. The roughness of the brush strokes tends to flatten down and disappear. Paint made with poppy oil, on the other hand, has usually a more buttery consistency. The surface of the brush stroke keeps its unevenness. The crests and hollows of the gobs of paint do not level out. The paint surface remains rough like plaster. This became even more pronounced when the manufacturer began to add waxes, metal soaps and other substances, sometimes even water, to their mixtures. These additions enabled the color merchants to make paint with more oil and less pigment—a great economy since the pigment is usually the more expensive of the two. Such adulterants also served to prevent pigment and oil from separating in the tube, and reduced even further the danger of the paint drying before it could be sold. With these additions paint could now be made without fear of premature drying, even with the cheaper linseed oil. And linseed oil, in fact, is what most manufacturers use today. On the other hand, these additions are not so advantageous to the painter. Paint made with them does not dry to as tough a film. Since the paint has less pigment in proportion to its bulk, it is less opaque and must be put on more thickly.

This new paint was not as satisfactory as the old for the sort of indirect painting the painters had been accustomed to doing. It dried too slowly. The poppy oil and the new adulterants made a slow-drying paint. A "dead painting" in this paint, thick enough to hide the grain of the canvas, took a long time to harden—all the more since the "dead color" was principally composed of black and white, and black pigments are the slowest to dry of all. Fresh paint laid over half-dried paint is sure to crack. So that, using the new slow-drying paints for the "dead painting" of a planned picture, the artist had to wait an inconveniently long time before he dared begin his second sitting.

On the other hand, the new paint was admirably adapted to a sort of painting where each tone is put down as it is intended to appear in the finished picture. Here slow drying is no disadvantage. It keeps the picture wet and malleable until the painter has finished with it. But oil paint is more transparent than anyone who had not worked with it can imagine. With the new adulterants it is more transparent still. So that in this "direct painting" the paint has to be put on thick, and if the color is to remain clean, the wet paint that is underneath must be disturbed or raked up as little as possible. Consequently the painter must work with large brushes of pig bristle. The brushes must be large—wet paint applied with small brushes on top of thick wet paint would give a troubled surface and a muddy tone; they must be made of pig bristle because the softer hair of the marten or sable (camel's hair as it is commonly misnamed) will not hold enough paint to give a loaded brush stroke. On the exploitation of this loaded brush stroke was founded perhaps the most influential, certainly the most prosperous, of all the schools of painting of the second half of the nineteenth century.

The virtuoso brush stroke was in itself not anything new in painting. As an independent display of skill, as an additional pattern imposed on the pattern of the picture, it has always been part of the painting tradition since the late Renaissance. Frans Hals, for example, in the north, and Salvator Rosa in the south, had used it for this purpose with considerable effect. But for the nineteenth century painters, the virtuoso brush stroke was not an adjunct. It was an essential part of their painting style and the distinguishing mark of their pictures. It became, in fact, so necessary that painters frequently faked it. They would first paint their pictures quite smoothly. Then—as Sargent in his early days is said to have done—they would scrape off the paint with a palette knife, and on top of the thin, smeared image left in the grain of the canvas, would repaint the picture,—to prove the originality, spontaneity, and dash of their genius—in bold, virtuoso brush strokes, each one carefully worked out in advance.

Another element, along with the practice of direct

painting from the model and the systematic use of the loaded brush, was the influence of Spanish painting—particularly of the painting of Velasquez which until this time was little known outside of Spain. According to Manet, there were at this time only two Velasquez in the Louvre, one of which—a standard Philip IV—was probably a school copy and not by the master's hand. We must remember that until late in the nineteenth century photographs of paintings did not exist. Pictures could be known only through inadequate engravings and more or less accurate copies, or by going and standing directly in front of the pictures themselves. To see Spanish painting one was obliged to go to Spain. And it was not until somewhere in the 1840's that it became easy for tourists to go there.

Spain in the sixteenth and seventeenth centuries was one of the richest and most advanced of the European nations, but travel within its borders was extremely difficult unless one had a great deal of money. Travel in France and Italy had always been fairly easy. There were good roads and inns in parts of France. Ever since the earliest times when convents, inns and shrines had been built at convenient distances along the roads to Rome for the use of pilgrims and crusaders, hotel keeping and the tourist trade had been among the most prosperous of Italian industries. But throughout the rest of Europe in the sixteenth and seventeenth centuries, travel was dangerous, expensive and extremely uncomfortable. In the eighteenth century, conditions improved. Post roads, and post horse services were organized, generally under government supervision, and anyone who wished to, could go almost anywhere—except, of course, to Spain. In Spain travel conditions were still practically those of the sixteenth century. There were few roads, few inns and little food. Travelers off the main roads had to go armed, accompanied by armed servants, carrying with them whatever they might need in the way of bedding and provisions, and in frequent danger of their lives. How difficult it was even as late as the early nineteenth century can be seen from George Borrow's account of his adventures in *The Bible in Spain*. It was not until the Carlist troubles were well over—somewhere in the 40's—that Spain became reasonably safe for tourists. Spain was wild, it was difficult of access. It was unlike any other part of Europe. Therefore the Romantics found it wonderful. Mérimée and Gautier went there. Alexandre Dumas and Delacroix passed through on their voyages to Algiers. Through these and other travelers the French painters learned about Spanish painting, and in particular about what they found to be the most remarkable of all, the painting of Velasquez. Manet himself did not get there until 1865, a number of years after he had begun painting Spanish subjects. He stayed in the first hotel in Madrid to be run in the European style, and like a good Parisian, complained bitterly about the food. But he had come and he remained because, like all the rest of the painters, he had been enormously impressed by Velasquez' naturalism.

Almost photographic naturalism was perhaps Velasquez' most astonishing quality, the complete detachment with which he regarded his sitter, the ability to put down on canvas exactly what was before his eyes. The painter took no part for or against the sitter. He was not awed by his model's grandeurs. He did not approve or disapprove. He did not even condone. He assumed no moral attitude whatever, even of pleasure. He kept his distance. From this distance he saw. He was the embodiment of the "scientific attitude." It was as if the painter were a sensitive mechanical contrivance able to record objectively the sitter's appearance without recourse to any human intervention, as if the painter were the perfect camera—a camera operating, not with the hesitations and accidents and inefficiencies of the usual application of scientific principles, but with the sureness, and resourcefulness and precision of the human mind.

As one can see, this notion of the camera occurs continually in nineteenth century painting. Photography was enormously interesting to everybody. So also was the "scientific attitude of mind" which had produced, and was producing still, so many marvels. It is not at all astonishing that the almost "scientific" detachment of Velasquez was so admired and imitated by these post-photographic painters.

Out of these elements—direct painting, the loaded brush and Velasquez—came the most successful school of painting of the nineteenth century. Its adherents were innumerable. Manet, Sargent, Chase, Sorolla, Zorn, Boldini, and Whistler are some of the better remembered. Their painting methods were quite unlike the painting methods of the official painters who considered themselves the inheritors of the classic tradition. Their aesthetic tone was on the whole "realistic," and in no way agreed with the debased romanticism of the official painters. But the technique of the virtuoso brush stroke proved so immediately successful, popular and teachable, that it was quickly adopted as a legitimate part of the academic tradition, and its practitioners became official, powerful and frequently rich.

There were of course troubles. Manet had plenty of them, not only on account of his painting methods, which were well in advance of his contemporaries, but also on account of differences in subject matter which to our eyes, with the change of times and fashions, are no longer new, shocking or even apparent. Sargent's *Madame X* and Manet's *Olympia* caused equal scandals and for similar reasons, less for the manner in which they were painted—that is to say with a loaded brush that followed the forms, and with great areas of black—than because both depicted an unaccustomed form of female elegance, and were consequently believed to have been intended as affronts to all respectable women. Manet, however, remains for us the more interesting. His pictures possess, as Sargent's do not, the hidden associations and multiple meanings which we today consider essential. These visual puns Manet's own time found extremely shocking. The *Déjeuner sur l'Herbe* outraged the public by the impudence of its classical references—to Giorgione's *Concert Champêtre* and to a well-known drawing by Raphael of river gods and nymphs. And the *Olympia* scandalized its own time, and still remains interesting to our own, because it is at the same time a superb painting and a successful parody, in the terms of 1870, of a Titian Venus—with a celebrated and recognizable Parisian cocotte for the Venus, a Negro maid instead of the white servant in the Titian picture, and in the place of the little dog, a black cat whose presence everyone, for some now incomprehensible reason, seemed to find particularly scandalous. But scandals such as these serve only to confirm the reputation of a style or a painter.

The center of the style was France, as it was for all the rest of nineteenth century painting, and Manet its most reputable exponent. But it was quickly internationalized. Even the small list of painters I have given contains three Americans, a Spaniard, an Italian and a Swede. For its practitioners, the style had every advantage. It was easily learned, easily understood by the public, brilliant in its effect, admired by the rich and respectable, and could be used for the production of large, imposing and salable pictures. What more could be asked?

Only, I am afraid, a more permanent immortality. It is not aging well. Even by the turn of the century the style had begun to appear somewhat vulgar. And today anyone who admits an admiration for these painters is considered either wilfully perverse or actually lacking in taste. Manet and Whistler, curiously enough, do not fall under the ban. It is partly on account of the real quality of their painting, but also, I suspect, for extra-artistic reasons as well—Manet on account of his connections with the Impressionists (one forgets how atrocious were the pictures he painted under Impressionist influence—all spinach green); and Whistler because of his lawsuit with Ruskin, in which he appears as a defender of a modern aesthetics, and because of his reputation as a wit. Today the insignificance of most of this painting is admitted without question by everybody, and for a number of good reasons.

To begin with, the paint itself in these pictures seems ugly to us. This is somewhat the fault of the commercially manufactured paint itself. It is chiefly due to the way the paint was used. The older painters painted only their light tones thick; their darks are always thin, or if not thin, at any rate transparent. These transparent darks are lively to begin with, and generally take on in aging an added warmth and richness. But in the pictures of the "brush stroke" school, the lights and darks are painted alike—with opaque paint and with a loaded brush. These thick and opaque darks are likely to be lifeless and heavy even when they are fresh, and time does not improve them.

Perhaps this is not important. We have no difficulty admiring other painters whose paint is not pretty. A more serious reason why these "brush stroke" pictures seem to us on the whole shallow and somewhat empty is the artificial method of drawing the painters used, a system of drawing derived directly from the optical theories of the camera.

The older, and to our eyes, more normal method of drawing, is tactile as much as it is visual. The painter tries first to understand the object to be drawn as something existing in space, as a solid body that can be felt with the hands or can be walked around. He uses his lights, shadows, colors, proportions, even textures of paint, as arbitrarily as he wishes, to represent the solid object on his canvas. He is at liberty to exaggerate the object's solidity or to flatten it down to a silhouette just as he needs or pleases. This is a question of composition, tact and convenience. But this method of drawing is, in its essentials, sculptural. The object is drawn as if it can be touched as well as seen.

The important element here is the arbitrary way the painter uses his means. The lights and darks he puts down are not necessarily the lights and darks that he himself sees in the object he is painting. They are instead the particular lights and darks which will cause a spectator to see the object as the painter wants it to be seen.

The method of drawing of the "brush stroke" painters, on the other hand, is purely visual, and takes the sense of touch little into account. It supposes that the eye is a machine like the camera without awareness of space or memory of the past. The object to be painted is first analyzed into shapes of light, half light, and shade. These shapes are then put on the canvas as similar shapes, in the same relative values of black and white, and of similar color. Shapes like this are the basis of photography. It is supposed that they are the basis of human vision as well; that when a spectator looks at the shapes on the canvas he will have before him everything the painter knew about the object he was painting. And that the painted shapes, reassembled in the spectator's eye, will form for him the exact image of the original object.

The difference between these two conceptions of drawing can be seen quite clearly in a recent documentary film on Michelangelo. Here the paintings shown seem much more solid than the statues. In the paintings, the painter himself had already used his lights and darks to underline the sculptural aspect of the forms he was presenting. The camera could imitate the lights and darks the painter had established and pass on to us what the painter had intended us to see. But when the camera was turned on the sculpture, it could only record a set of merely accidental lights and darks, and these it could not point up—as can a painter—to demonstrate the statues' solid forms. So that in the film, the paintings looked solid by the painter's own intention. But whatever solidity the statues seemed to have was there only by accident and implication. It was not until the camera moved, and an extra dimension was added by its motion to its vision, that the statues appeared as solid as the paintings.

Actually, a purely visual approach to drawing gives a highly simplified picture of the world. It is, to use a term from metaphysics, "subjective." The painter attempts to record only his own optical sensations. It is not necessary for him to take into account the real existence of the object he is drawing. His mind is supposed to receive only the sensations a photographic plate could register. The painter and his model do not touch. He does not have to know his model's solid being. By disregarding its extension in space, the object is deprived of much of its emotional force, and the painter, by limiting himself only to what he sees, is enabled to keep his detachment, his necessary "scientific attitude," and can avoid any personal involvement whatsoever. This, as one can readily see, is an enormous advantage in portrait painting.

But all this has its disadvantages also. It gives but a limited description of objects in space. It attributes to them only the dimensions of right-and-left and up-and-down. Whereas objects as we actually encounter them are also far-and-near in distance, and before-and-after in time. This makes four dimensions to be taken into account. But even four is not enough. We ourselves are also objects and can move around among the other objects space contains. So that to make our description of space complete, and to explain why the shape of objects seems to change as we move among them, we need, I have been told, three more dimensions as well to describe our position as separate from the things we move among. This would bring the number of terms necessary to describe the space we live in up to seven, more, probably, than the painter needs. But it is true that the painter who limits himself to the optical method of drawing and its two dimensions robs what he is painting of most of its emotional effect. The optical method of drawing deprives the outside world of much of its actuality and can never exert the emotional power of the more flexible, tactile, almost sculptural, sort of drawing the older painters practiced.

No one, of course, ever followed this system of drawing to extremes. It is quite impossible to draw anything without taking into account something of its solidity. But, as much as it is possible to do so, the "brush stroke" painters describe an optical rather than a tangible world. The painter does not move among the objects he is painting. He is instead a one-eyed observer looking at nature through a peephole. This simplification helps explain the shallowness of many of these painters' pictures. It also helps explain the surprising ease and brilliance with which they were executed.

The rest of this brilliance is due to the use of a technical trick we now find very distasteful—the brush stroke that follows the form. This is to say that a painter painting, for example, an arm, puts down the lights, half lights and shadows, and perhaps even the background behind it, as stripes of paint applied with a brush following the arm's outline. The outline itself is often the ridge of paint left piled up by the side of the brush against the background. This is a technical device which gives the appearance of great brilliance without much effort. In these painters it is endlessly repeated. Sargent, Zorn and even Manet are full of it. The brilliance of Boldini—perhaps the most brilliant of them all—is arrived at by an almost exclusive use of this device. For example there is his picture in the Metropolitan in which the Duchess of Marlborough and her son seem to float in a sea of gracious worldliness, and where each entwined finger is apparently painted with a single motion of the brush.

I am not certain why we today find this mannerism so distasteful. Perhaps because it is so easy to do. Perhaps because it so quickly became a formula of the schools. Perhaps because the hardness of the edges it invariably gives drains air out of the picture and brings the image too close to the surface of the canvas. Perhaps because the all too evident motion of the painter's brush follows and overemphasizes the picture's linear pattern. But whatever the reason may be, the brush stroke that follows the form is an easy and brutal effect, never employed by the older painters, not even to any extent by Frans Hals, the great master of virtuosity.

Apart from this troublesome brilliance, another thing that bothers us about these pictures is their size. They seem much too large. To us, with the smaller scale of our domestic architecture, apartments and arrangements, and with the smaller scale of our private living, the size and scale that seems normal in a picture is that of an Impressionist landscape—a picture small enough to have been carried on the painter's back or under his arm to the spot where he was painting, and consequently small enough to hang in an ordinary living room. As one can see even from this most commonplace example, the size of a picture determines both the conditions under which it can be painted and the use to which it can be put. Small pictures can be hung or painted anywhere. Large pictures like those of the "brush stroke" painters require large studios for their making and must be looked at in large halls. Not only this, but the complexity and amount of detail in a picture, as well as its size, must also be quite different depending on whether the picture is intended for public or for private use.

Pictures for private houses do not always have to be small, although they generally are, but they must always have a rich and complex surface. They are to be seen often and near. They must be complex enough to continue to hold the attention, and detailed enough to look well from close at hand. Pictures for large halls or for a public show have quite different requirements. The painter must aim at carrying power, not complexity. The picture is to be seen perhaps only once and from a considerable distance. Its purpose is to seize the attention, not to hold it. Such a picture must be large, simple and clear in construction, and economical in detail. It must be painted, in short, in the manner whose final exaggeration is used to produce the poster and the billboard.

This difference between public and private pictures is one we are very conscious of today. It is a distinction the painters of the visible "brush stroke" school did not observe. The great mass of their pictures, even those intended for private homes, seem today suitable only for public exhibition, and consequently appear to us more than a little blatant and empty.

We must remember, however, that the visible "brush

stroke" school was the most successful, the most advanced in technique and the least offensive in taste of all the official painting of the time. It was also the most expensive. The ten thousand dollar portrait was not uncommon. These pictures were bought in great quantities, ordered by contracts as detailed and specific as the theatrical contracts of the present day. It was a time of large houses and large receptions. The immense rooms in which these pictures hung differed little in size from the exhibition galleries in which they were first displayed. They were painted to be looked at from a certain distance, with a consequent brutality of contrasts, display of brushwork and suppression of subtleties and details that do not suit at all the smaller apartments and the more intimate social sets and private living we now esteem. Our intellectual fashions and artistic ideals come no longer from sets and families dedicated to the management of wealth or government, who use parade in the daily business of their living. They come instead from the private-minded middle classes. Consequently we are shocked by what we consider the pictures' ostentation and shallowness.

It is about time, however, to make some sort of re-evaluation of the "brush stroke" painters. We complain that their color is dull; perhaps, compared with their contemporaries the Impressionists, it is. But the Impressionists' pictures are holding their bright colors less well than we imagine; many of them have already become as drab as Bouguereau. And taste in color changes. The neon colors of the plastics are already causing a reaction. Black, brown, beige, gray, dull blue and smoky green are coming into their own again—exactly the colors (with perhaps a spot of vermilion added somewhere to make them "sing") which so many of these "brush stroke" pictures have concealed beneath their yellowed varnish. We complain about the simplicities of character depicted in the innumerable portraits. Nevertheless these cheerful, clean-cut young men, these serene girls, these innocent and confident matrons, these kindly financiers most certainly existed. They are the precise faces described in the novels of Henry James, and I am surprised that some publisher has not already issued an edition of James's works with Sargent's portraits for illustrations.

As technicians, too, some of these painters are better than we nowadays care to admit, and not really unworthy of being associated with Manet and Whistler. There are, for instance, in Sorolla, tricks in the rendering of water, and of light and wetness on sunburned flesh, that any painter would wish to be able to do. As for Manet himself, no one has anything but the highest praise for his ability as a painter or for the quality of his mind. In fact the work of Manet is so esteemed that he is classed among the Impressionists, where he in no way belongs, to protect him from the odium attached to the painters of the "brush stroke" school. There is no charge of vulgarity against Whistler either, although Whistler cannot by any stretch of definition be attached to Impressionism. Whistler was perhaps a painter of less technical ability than some of the others. But he was a man of intellectual distinction, an innovator and a colorist. His experiments with the then fashionable Japanese system of composition seem to us rather unfortunate. But his interest in color harmonies, which on account of the treacherous materials he seems to have used have almost all disappeared, give his pictures a restraint and elegance lacking in most of the other "brush stroke" painters.

That we approve of a few of these painters is a detail —an accident of our fashion and their own individual talent —and not enough to justify the school. That must be done on the subject matter of the pictures. We may not find the subject matter of these painters as interesting as that of their contemporaries the Impressionists. But however much it may have been at times degraded for fashionable or for official uses, the subject matter of these "brush stroke" painters was, after all, Realism. As such it is infinitely more interesting to us than the sentimental sensuality and debased Romanticism of the right wing conservatives—the Salon of Monsieur Bouguereau as Cézanne called them—who throughout the last part of the nineteenth century held all the official positions and considered themselves, in spite of their tired color and labored drawing, the heirs of the great tradition. And well they may have been; so little of it any longer existed.

CHAPTER SIX

THE SECOND REVOLUTION

We have seen book cases that were superb works of art. The mouldings carved in fine leaf ornaments; the pilasters were knights in full armor; the panels, hunting scenes; and the cornice surmounting the whole, a perfect confusion of guns, pistols, swords, spears and arms—the whole carved in solid oak and dyed a dark color, without polish, so as to resemble time-worn wood. The effect is grand. A dining-room, where the panels of the sideboard are of game or fish, and the top is a fine elk or boar's head, and other parts ornamented in the same style, is antique and stylish. Poor imitations of this furniture should be avoided, as the only thing that reconciles correct taste to this *outré* character of furniture is the artistic execution of the sculpture. It must be a work of art (although the figures may not represent anything on the earth), and all imitations are but buffoonery. The dragon's head is a favorite ornament for the arms of a chair or sofa, a lion's claw for the foot, and a serpent coiled fantastically for the back. In the hands of good designers, this style is prolific in subjects for the pencil, and a room furnished correctly in this manner is very grand and imposing, and will endure the ravages of time.

Sloan's Homestead Architecture, by Samuel Sloan, Architect (Philadelphia, 1870).

If the school of the virtuoso brush stroke was the left wing of official painting of the last quarter of the nineteenth century, the right wing—the die-hard conservatives—was the school of no brush stroke at all. These were even more numerous than the others. Gérôme, Meissonier, Fortuny, Cabanel, Bouguereau, Couture (who was Manet's master) are some of them. But most of the names we have forgotten. It is partly because of the intense distaste we feel for the sentimental Romanticism which was the subject of their pictures. It is chiefly because their painting methods went out of style, rendered obsolete by the Impressionists.

These methods, the painters of the no-brush-stroke school derived from the eighteenth century painters, whose inheritors they considered themselves to be. To the eighteenth century system, they added as an extra gentility the smooth, enamel surface which Ingres before them had perfected. They began by making a complete painting in black and white, not a rough beginning like the eighteenth century "dead painting," but a complete, smooth picture, as detailed in black and white as the finished picture would eventually be in color. When dry, this underpainting was repainted in the proper colors. Unlike the eighteenth century system, great care was taken to leave no brush stroke visible, no mark of the human hand. For it was the absence of just such human imperfections which identified the painter as a Poet and a Genius. Photography, you see, pops up again, but with this difference: here the painter is not a camera. He is an art photographer tinting a photograph.

This particular method of painting, however, with its insistent precision, was invented long before photography. David and the other "Classicists" had already used it for their own purposes. For these painters, the greatest art was that of Greece and Rome, and the noblest possible achievement of artistic expression was a group of classical statues illustrating some moral incident from Plutarch. Classical sculpture as we ourselves know it, was, on account of the English blockade, unknown to David and his school. The masterpieces of antiquity, for them, were the late, and somewhat inferior productions—the Farnese Hercules, the Medici Venus, the Laocoön, and the Belvedere Apollo. Nevertheless the admiration of these painters for classical antiquity was so great that they considered the most important part of painting to be the part which might be made to resemble such Graeco-Roman sculpture. Consequently the part of a picture on which they took the greatest pains was its preparation in black and white, which, with its lack of color, might call to mind something of these statues' unadorned nobility. So that the figures in their pictures were first completed in the color (and sometimes even in the lack of costume) of a plaster cast. Only afterwards were they clothed and colored—and that in obedience to what these painters thought of as a local and distinctly barbarian prejudice.

It was Ingres, however, who brought this painting method to its final perfection. Just as David had epitomized the nobility of political revolt and the republican virtues, the painting of Ingres contains all the solid fabrics and middle-class comforts of the reign of Louis Philippe, the king who carried an umbrella. Ingres's clear, untroubled color on top of the skillfully rounded edges of his underpainting makes his pictures marvels of harmony, softness and respectability.

But in the hands of the official painters of the nineteenth century, the method worked less well. Ingres had had no difficulty with it. He drew so easily that the carefully shaded edges of his underpainting cost him no effort at all. And for the eighteenth century painters, the "dead painting" had been only a foundation, a useful guide, a sketch to be elaborated as the picture grew, the easiest way a picture could be begun. But the method these late nineteenth century painters used was not easy at all. Each picture had to be finished twice, once in black and white to imitate a photograph, and once in color to imitate art.

It takes a subject of some importance to accept such labor. A painter has only a limited amount of energy at his disposal for the execution of an idea, and the amount of energy depends on how interesting the idea is. In fact, the importance of an idea can usually be judged by the amount of labor it can, with grace, accept. Somewhere in the middle of this laborious system these painters had adopted, this painful finishing and subsequent tinting of pictures whose ideas were of no real interest to anybody, the painter would discover that he had lost his ability to see. His invention was gone. His picture was finished in ugly tones of battleship gray. And he had no idea what to do next.

In such a case the tricks of color and of drawing learned at school will sometimes patch up a picture enough for it to be shown. But the picture will always be labored and unconvincing. This is without doubt what must have happened to the Gérôme in the Metropolitan Museum, where Galatea, a putty-colored statue of a female nude, is blushing into a pink life which has not yet reached the buttocks, under Pygmalion's ardent and astonished gaze. The painter had set a bear trap to catch a mouse. The trap was sprung, but the mouse was gone.

With other of these painters the system worked better, and many of the pictures will become, with our next change of taste, justly admired and unquestionably handsome. But all of these painters got into trouble when they had to deal with official poetry. Since they were official painters, patronized by the government and attached to the academies, official poetry was for the most part what they had to deal with. And the official poetry of the late nineteenth century was a lady-like and well-behaved Romanticism.

The Romantic movement was originally no such milk-and-water proposition. It had begun as a violent reaction against the restrictions of eighteenth century French taste and manners. Romanticism insisted that man was more interesting in his natural and violent aspects than in the limiting disguise of the decorum he used for appearing in a drawing room—which, after all, as Leibnitz I believe said, is only a limited portion of infinite space. The admiration of the Romantics for the wild, the tumultuous, the untrammeled, in man and in nature, had freed both the writers and the painters from some tiresome conventions of style and from some absurd canons of criticism. For the writer and poet, it furnished an immense new subject matter. For the painter it provided a new aspect of man and of nature. But the painter is not a wanderer. Because of the very conditions of his trade he cannot afford to lead the adventurous life of a Romantic poet. His materials are too cumbersome. He cannot go far afield to find these new aspects of man and nature, or if he does, the most he can carry with him is his sketch book. If he wishes to paint big, impressive pictures with Romantic subjects, he had best provide himself with vicarious experiences from the specialists in these matters—either take his subjects from the Romantic poets themselves and from the writers the Romantics admired, or else illustrate the far distant events in exotic settings which the poets found politically significant. Otherwise the painter was liable to fall into such absurdities of Romantic realism as Courbet's huge self portrait, where Courbet himself is shown on a country road, life size in hiking clothes with a pack on his back, being greeted by two peasants, hats in hand, and which bears the title—believe it or not—of "*Bonjour Monsieur Courbet.*" All this is too preposterous to be anything except a painter's own naïve idea of an allegory, perhaps something like Art being Respected by the People, and certainly very unprofessional from a poetic point of view.

The Romantic poets were safer guides to subject matter than this. Long before Romanticism had become the official philosophy of the French government, Delacroix, Romantic revolutionary, had painted *Hamlet and the*

Grave Diggers and *Lady Macbeth* (as the play is called in French) after Shakespeare, and *The Giaour*, *The Bride of Abydos*, and *Don Juan's Shipwreck* after Byron (just as the equally unofficial Romantic composer Berlioz had taken for subjects *A Midsummer Night's Dream* and *The Damnation of Faust*). Géricault's *Raft of the Medusa* had caused such scandal by its anti-governmental implications that the title of the picture had to be changed for exhibition and the name of the ship left out.

But all this was while Romanticism was still the movement of revolt. By the time of Napoleon III and commercial photography Romanticism had lost its violence. It was still the painters' subject matter, but it had become respectable, official and verbose. A painting could tell a story. In these days before the motion pictures, telling a story was a thing photography could not easily do, and photography had become the official painters' particular rival. So the official painters told stories, and official painting became little else than illustrations of sentimental and romantic themes. After Romantic subjects from the poets, the painters took exotic subjects (Algerian, Turkish, Egyptian), historical subjects (Greek, Roman, Early Christian, Medieval), sentimental subjects (*A Stolen Kiss*, *The Warrior's Farewell*), and finally any subject at all (*Apotheosis of the Poet*, *The Witches' Sabbath*, *The Sleeping Nymph*) which gave the painter an excuse to exhibit the pretty bottoms of pretty girls, bottoms which seem to have had the same safe and public significance in the erotic vocabulary of the late nineteenth century that up-standing breasts possess today.

These painters were unbelievably industrious. The pictures they painted were many, elaborate and frequently enormous. *The Romans of the Decadence* for example, of Couture, which I suppose is still in the Louvre, presents an immense marble hall with columns, containing I do not know how many decadent Romans, all with Roman robes, wreaths and hangovers. Meissonier's battle pieces have innumerable horses and heroes. Bouguereau's satyrs are permitted to gaze with rapture and edification on innumerable nymphs. The acres of canvas which Doré, the popular illustrator of Dante's *Inferno*, covered with warm, unpleasant color cannot be counted. The works of the Romantic poets these official painters illustrated, and the works of the officially successful writers and musicians, who were these painters' contemporaries, remain some of the finest productions of the nineteenth century. This literature and music is not so different from our own. But when we look at the official painting, it seems incredible to us that anyone could have gone to the labor either of painting it or liking it. For we are separated from this academic painting, this official poetry, by a revolution in taste and in the technique of painting as complete as the revolution caused by the invention of painting in oil.

How complete was this revolution can be seen in the contemptuous meaning we now lend the word "academic." To call a painter "academic" is today the greatest possible insult. But for these right wing official painters of the late nineteenth century, it was with considerable satisfaction, and even pride, that they thought of themselves as the inheritors of the academic tradition. Academic, meaning attached to an academy, carried with it for them all the honorable associations connected with Plato's Academy and the groves in which it met. "Academic" was never, before the middle of the nineteenth century, a term of reproach. Ever since the Academy of Bologna had been founded in 1585 by the Carracci for teaching painting, and painting had become something students in a school paid to be taught instead of something apprentices in a workshop got paid to learn, a good painter was likely to be an academician. That is to say that he would be attached to a school, a painting academy—as Le Sueur and Chardin were attached to the Academie des Beaux Arts, or Reynolds and Turner to the Royal Academy—partly from the pleasure and profit to be got from association with their fellow painters, partly for the privilege of showing their pictures in the members' expositions, but principally as a painting instructor for the young. In fact, the painters teaching at the New York Art Students' League, although they have no official prerogatives, form just such an academy today. The painter thus distinguished was expected to pass on to his students the best—that is to say the academic—traditions of his art.

The Academic tradition, as I have already pointed out, was principally concerned with the planned picture. All the academic devices of underpainting, color theory, composition, anatomy, drawing from nude models and painting from these drawings, historical research in costume, literary research in the classics, and so on, which are still taught at the Academie des Beaux Arts in Paris, had as their sole end the production of a planned picture with a subject. Even today in Paris, a student competing for the *Prix de*

Rome in painting, is shut up "*en loge*," in a studio with a bed, food, paints, canvas, access to books and models, and a subject (*Caesar on the Rubicon*, *Achilles in His Tent*, *The Death of Cleopatra*) and is expected to paint without help and in a given time a picture by which his merits as a painter can be judged. Since the academic devices were designed precisely for turning out these elaborately planned pictures with a subject, the planned picture could lend itself all too easily to anecdote and official poetry. And this, of course, it did. It is perhaps not the fault of the academies that official poetry of the nineteenth century went bad. But the academies did very little to prevent it. Even when such magnificent painters as David and Ingres were at the head of the Beaux Arts, the official poetry the Academy and the salons endorsed was none too good (like the official poetry of Napoleon's coronation both of these painters illustrated). After Ingres official poetry was atrocious. Noble Romans, cardinals drinking wine, Fausts and Marguerites, Uncle Tobies and Widow Wadmans, Arab slave marts, coy nymphs and satyrs out on a spree, scenes of domestic life, of children, of dogs, of soldiers, that filled the official salons are not good subjects for pictures, nor would it have been possible to have made good pictures from them. They have nothing to do with the painter's private view of the world and his own mind, out of which alone good pictures can be made. They are not even interesting as stories. Their sentimental Romanticism is as false and official as the sentimental Realism of our own movies. These, nevertheless, were the subjects of the pictures accepted by the salons and awarded prizes. For just as our own movie-makers believe that middle-class life, when glamourized by photography, becomes in some mysterious way interesting, these painters were convinced that an anecdote, no matter how silly, could be dignified by painting into art.

We today have no idea how bad these pictures were. We have not seen them. The museums which once bought them or accepted them as gifts are ashamed to hang them, or even to admit they still preserve them in their cellars. When they come up at public auction they are knocked down for the dubious value of their gold and plaster frames. Few students of nineteenth century painting know them even as photographs. But what we all do know is that after Ingres, no painter we admire today belonged to an official academy. The living tradition of our painting is the tradition of revolt. For us a painter who receives official sanction is under grave suspicion, because, after Corot and until Picasso, not a single painter whose work has had any influence on our taste or painting received official recognition during his lifetime from these academic circles, or was anything but a scandal to them. It is on this account that "academic painter" has come to mean "bad painter," and it is here that the Impressionist revolt begins. It is the Impressionist revolution which is the source of all the painting of the present day.

We are accustomed to think of Impressionism as the theory of broken color, as a revolt against the brown sauces of the academic painters. But the Impressionist revolt was more profound than this. It was a revolt against the anecdote, and even against the planned picture itself. The Impressionists threw overboard the whole body of academic tradition. The great scandal of their painting was not that their pictures were bright but that they were unpremeditated.

Improvisatory painting was not entirely new. It had been practiced as early as the middle of the eighteenth century. There is a nude of Fragonard inscribed on the back of the canvas "Frago painted this in an hour." Some of the pictures of Guardi, of Tiepolo, and the smaller pictures of Constable are certainly improvisations. But throughout the eighteenth century the distinctions were maintained. Improvisations were understood to be sketches. Real pictures took planning. But with the Impressionists this difference disappeared. The sketch became the picture. And the big picture—which always takes a certain time to paint—became a series of sketches superimposed one on top the other.

Here is a curious anomaly. Degas, in my opinion the most consistently successful of all the Impressionists (I have seen bad Monets, Manets, Renoirs, Cézannes and Pissarros; I have never seen a bad Degas) was not an improvisatory painter and consequently not an Impressionist at all. Perhaps it is because he left so many unfinished pictures that he is classed among the Impressionists. All these drawings, pastels, oils, figures in sculpture, small and large canvases in the most advanced Impressionist colors and techniques are nevertheless only sketches. They are the designs and material intended to be used for the production of small planned pictures with subjects, in the most correct academic tradition and in the no-brush-stroke style. Whereas the proper strict Impressionist painter placed himself before his motif, and on a blank canvas without a plan, painted his picture as casually as if he were pointing his camera and snapping the shutter.

The most striking characteristic of the Impressionist pictures is perhaps their cool, their blue or violet, general tone. It is partly that the Impressionists disdained the orange-tinted varnish "soups" the official painters used to give their own work a false age and a museum respectability. But it is chiefly the accidental result of the Impressionists' habit of painting out-of-doors. Shadow tones out-of-doors, on the bright days when painters work, are likely to be blue or violet. And it is the color of the shadows, not of the lights, which determines the general color tone of a picture.

The official painters painted indoors, if possible in a studio with windows facing north so that the sun could not enter or the direction of the light on the model change. North light is blue. Even on a cloudy day it is relatively cool. The color of a studio itself is generally warm. That is to say that the color of its walls, floors, hangings and other furniture is more likely to be in the browns and reds and oranges than in the lilacs, grays or blues. Consequently a model posed in a studio will be lighted by a cold light; and the shadows, which reflect the warm tones of the room, will be reddish, brown or orange. Even when such a painter painted out-of-doors, he was more likely than not to execute his picture in the tonality he had been accustomed to use for indoor painting, just as if the landscape had been brought into the studio and lighted with the usual studio lighting of warm shadows and cool lights.

The Impressionists, on the other hand, painted out-of-doors on principle. Sunlight is yellow or orange. The blue of the sky gives blue reflections in the shadows of near-by objects, and the blue color of the air gives a blue cast to all distant things, so that the only warm colors in the Impressionists' landscapes are the brightly lighted parts of the objects in the foreground. All the rest of the picture is in violets, greens and blues. Even when the Impressionist painted indoors, he was likely to look for, find, and paint, if not warm lights, at any rate blue shadows, and to exaggerate them. Vuillard, of course, worked almost entirely indoors, and consequently used a great deal of brown. But with the other Impressionists, a cool tonality and blue or lilac shadows became a trade mark and the easiest way to distinguish their work from the painters of the official schools.

In one respect, all these painters were alike. Different as the color system of the rebel Impressionists may have been from that of the official and academic painters, all the post-photographic painters are equally dependent on some aspect of photography. They differ only in the kind of photography each employs. The no-brush-stroke painter takes glossy prints and tints them. The virtuoso-brush-stroke painter manipulates a large, slow, expensive plate camera in a photographer's studio, using time exposures, arranged lighting and a portrait lense. The Impressionist wanders about the woods and fields with the new, fast, portable, inexpensive, daylight-loading, snapshot apparatus. Certain of the Impressionists, I have heard, even went to the trouble of having made large camera shutters through which they could look, and by painting only what they could see while the shutter was open, thought to reproduce more exactly the effect of an instantaneous exposure.

The Impressionist camera is loaded with color film. In fact, color photography and the Impressionists' broken color are both derived from the same source—the new theories of color vision and color mixing which the physicists had just recently formulated. The principles on which the first practical system of color photography was based had already been sketched out by Ducos du Hauron as early as 1868, only six years before the first Impressionist exposition. The first successful commercial application of these principles, the Autochrome process (in which the photograph is taken on a plate covered by a mixture of starch grains dyed three primary colors) differs little either in theory or appearance from the paintings of Monet or Pissarro. However, the Autochrome plate did not appear on the market until the first decade of the twentieth century. By this time the public had become accustomed to Impressionist painting, and could accept without question the somewhat coarse spottiness which the large color granulations of the Autochrome process give to the appearance of nature. So that perhaps we have here an example of what in our own time is more common than the influence of photography on painting—a contrariwise example of the influence of the painter on the camera.

Monet, Pissarro, Vuillard, Sisley, Bonnard, and Guillaumin followed the Impressionist theories fairly consistently. Vuillard so consistently that in his enormous interiors with people, the violent patterns of the wallpapers he painted are a great deal easier to see than the people hidden in front of them, which is of course exactly what happens to people in a room with wallpapers such as these. Few of the other Impressionists painted with such photographic accuracy. Cézanne used outline, solid forms and arbitrarily imposed compositions. Renoir, for sentimental effects, placed quite unphotographic accents, like round black shoe buttons, in the eyes of his little girls. Van Gogh's brush strokes followed the forms. His enormous reputation with a great public which has ordinarily no interest in pictures is proof enough of the excitement and vulgar appeal that an exaggeration of this particular mannerism can add to painting. Van Gogh's work, however, has exerted little influence on painters other than the German Expressionists, who were after all principally interested in excitement in painting. He has had nowhere else an influence comparable to the other painters who followed the Impressionist theory somewhat more exactly.

The Impressionist theory, with which we are all familiar, is that the painter is a disinterested spectator. His eye is pure. Like the camera, his eye has no preferences. Each element in the field of its vision is of equal importance in forming the image it sees. The painter aims his eye like a camera at the thing he is to paint and records the variations of light his eye receives in terms of spots of color. For the Impressionist, the world he paints is the world of the eye's sensations.

A painter in the classical tradition, on the other hand, considers the primary reality to be the object's solid form, which intercepts the light and casts a shadow. For the traditional painter a light cannot exist without a shadow. The presence of the one implies the other. But for the Impressionist, the primary reality is the sensation in his eye.

What he is painting is not form but light. One light cannot exist without another. The presence of a light does not imply a shadow. It implies the presence of another, different light. Consequently, his tones of paint do not represent chiaroscuro or light and dark. They represent, all of them, lights—lights of different strengths and colors, but none the less lights. Each tone, even a tone of deepest shadow, stands for a colored light. Each spot of colored light is of equal importance in producing in the painter's eye the sensation of the object he is painting. Since each square centimeter of painted canvas is to represent a light, each square centimeter of the finished picture must have an equal weight and an equal importance. Thus each square centimeter of the canvas must be painted with a similar, a carefully equalized, texture.

An equalized painted surface such as this cannot be got by any of the methods the official painters used. The virtuoso brush stroke which copies the shapes of lights and shadows in thick paint will not achieve it. The sharp edges of the brush strokes interfere. They are too important. The weights and tensions they add to the painted surface cannot be equally distributed. Nor will the laborious system of concealing the marks of the brush and painting with no apparent brush stroke at all do it either. In such painting one part of the picture will invariably be more detailed than another, and the surface of the picture at that point, in consequence, more labored. The Impressionists solved the problem and arrived at an equalized surface by adopting a neutral brush stroke, each one approximately the same size and shape, done with small brushes all the same size. The brush stroke never changes sizes or shape or inclination to fit the size of the detail being painted. It never at any time follows the direction of the shape of the painted forms. The painter uses his brush to make an extra pattern superimposed on the pattern of the picture and independent of the objects that are in it. Monet dabs. Pissarro scatters confetti. Seurat plants polka dots. Cézanne, in certain of his periods, adopts a diagonal twill. Thus by stylizing the brush stroke and painting everything in the picture in the same way, the objective clarity of the painter's impression of nature is not obscured by any mannerism of hand or handling.

This painted surface with equal tension in all its parts is the second of the Impressionists' great inventions. It was devised to represent more closely the camera's vision. We have taken it over for our own uses. It is to the Impressionists and their practices that we owe our present-day aesthetic of the equalized surface tension, of continuous surface without accent, on which is based all the good building, painting, design and even music of our time, from jet planes and pictures to soap boxes and swing.

It was the Impressionist revolution of 1870, and not the Cubist revolution of 1910, which was responsible for Modern Art. The Cubist revolution brought nothing new to the technique of painting. It brought only a new subject matter, already foreseen in the parodies of Manet, and executed in the accepted style of the improvised picture, with the continuous and equalized surface, already developed by the Impressionists. It is to Impressionism that we owe not only our liberation from a moribund Romanticism, but also the invention of the techniques and the establishment of the traditions of the painting of our time.

CHAPTER SEVEN

COLORS AND COLOR

> I have had occasion to remark that sober colors, employed in large pictures, produce great richness.
>
> Thomas Sully, *Hints to Young Painters*

The painter depends on the poet, the chemist and the physicist a great deal more than he likes to admit. He eagerly adopts the subjects the poets propose, the pigments the chemists invent and the theories of perspective and light the physicists devise, and turns them to his own uses. The Impressionist painters themselves were perhaps less dependent on the poets and literary men than is generally the case. Zola's painter hero in *L'Oeuvre*, for example, who killed himself because he could not finish a picture, aroused only their amused disdain. A real painter, as Cézanne pointed out, would have found it more advantageous to have begun another picture instead. But if the Impressionists found little inspiration in poetry itself, the poetry of applied science, on the other hand, they found extremely useful. Indeed the whole originality of the Impressionists derives from the scientific progress of their time—from a new theory of color mixing which they made their own, and from the new bright colors they used to expound it—from the most recent findings of physics and chemistry which were ready at hand when the Impressionists began to paint.

But with all their bright new colors, the Impressionists' pictures were never as bright as the old masters', nor were they, in fact, ever intended to be. They were only meant to be bright and clear. The Impressionists' pictures seemed startlingly bright to their contemporaries, not because their colors were bright but because they were unexpected. The Impressionists put their bright colors in places where painters had been in the habit of putting no color at all. They painted lavender and green in the shadows where gray or brown had always been used before. They got the effect of black with dark red and green and blue. They put bright blue in the shadows of snow and green in the shadows of hair. They were attempting to represent the effects of light, even to paint light itself. They wished the paint in their pictures to look like light instead of paint. As a consequence they painted in a very light, pale key, with a great deal of white mixed with all the colors. Colors in such pale, light tones have little power; the addition of white dulls a pigment as much as the addition of gray. In fact, white is nothing but the palest possible gray, and a purple, a green, and a blue which in their deeper tones are impossible to confuse, can become with the addition of white so muted as to be indistinguishable one from another. So that the Impressionists' pictures, with some exceptions of course, are seldom as brightly colored as we suppose or as we remember them to be.

The older painters of the sixteenth and seventeenth centuries never considered that they were painting with light. They had few bright colors and preferred to use them in the deeper tonal ranges where these pigments could be shown at their highest intensity and beauty. Their one bright red was vermilion. If a bright red coat was to be painted, the lights and darks of the rest of the picture would be so graded that the vermilion could be used pure. Any touch of black or white thrown in to adjust the pigment's tone would mar its brilliance. If a more scarlet hue than the orange of vermilion was needed for the coat, the painter would add yellow to all the other colors in the picture. Thus the general yellow tone of the rest of the picture would make the red-orange flame of the vermilion seem a scarlet red. A picture with much blue sky would be painted dark enough so that the costly ultramarine could be exhibited at its greatest beauty, as can be seen, for example, in the sky of Titian's *Rape of Europa* in Boston. These older painters considered that their pigments were only substances, with precise character and limited possibilities, and used every trick they knew to set them off to their best advantage. They knew that too many bright colors in a picture neutralized one another. The most brilliant effects were to be had with one or two bright colors set off by duller ones. Their few vivid pigments, used pure and thrown into relief against a neutral background, make their pictures very bright indeed. Look at certain of Velasquez' paintings, apparently executed with only white, black, brown and vermilion, or the superb Veronese in the

Ringling Museum, where the Holy Family, resting under a palm tree, is being tended by hovering angels. The colors in the picture appear astonishingly bright. Actually the only pigment used at its full intensity is the blue in the sky. Tiepolo was especially skillful at this sort of effect, where a robe, apparently a deep rich red, can only be matched, as anyone who has tried to copy one of his pictures knows, by a sort of reddish mud.

But the Impressionists were not painting pictures of colored objects. They were interested in a more complicated problem—what colored objects look like under colored light. Their palette was vastly richer than the older painters'. They had what none of the older painters possessed, mauves, violets, bright greens, oranges and intense yellows. They could allow themselves the liberty of forgetting that their pigments were only substances. They could permit themselves to confuse the paint on their palettes with the light they were attempting to represent. Operating with the new theory of the additive mixture of colors, which was based on the behavior of mixtures of colored lights, the Impressionists put down their dots of paint as if they were speckling the canvas with spots of colored light. These dots of paint were as far as possible pure, unmixed colors, nor were they blended on the canvas. They were intended to be mixed in the spectator's eye, where they were to produce the effect, not of a painting, but of an open window.

Whatever color theory the older painters had possessed was based only on the behavior of the mixture of pigments. Its principal function was to name and classify the colors of the objects in nature and to find out with what mixture of pigments these colors could be reproduced. There are, for example, color treatises of the eighteenth century which list in parallel columns the names of the colors (dove gray, lemon yellow, emerald green); samples of these colors in water color; the names of the pigments of which the samples are made; and where in nature (the breast of a dove, a ripe lemon, the head of a mallard duck) the colors themselves are to be found. The basis for this system was the three colors considered by these theorists to be the essential primaries—red, yellow and blue. The bright pigments available to them in these colors—carmine, gamboge and real ultramarine—were not, of course, the perfect primaries. But it was nevertheless believed that if three perfect primary pigments could be found, all other colors could be derived from their mixture.

This theory seemed satisfactory enough until it was discovered that none of it accounted for what happens when colored lights are mixed, and a new color theory had to be developed. It is this theory on which Impressionism is based. The new theory explained that there are two sorts of color mixtures—by addition and by subtraction, depending on whether the colors are mixed as substances or as lights. The two sorts of mixtures sometimes give quite different results. Take for example the mixture of yellow and blue, and let us mix a can of yellow with a can of blue paint. The color of a mixture of paint is governed by the same principles which control the color of the light passing through a stack of colored glass plates. Only that part of the spectrum can get through which all the glasses possess in common; the rest is blocked out. In the case of our blue and yellow paint, the yellow reflects, as we now know, both red and green as well as yellow; the blue both green and violet as well as blue. The color of their mixture will come from only the parts of the spectrum both reflect—which is green. So that, as we already know, a blue paint mixed with yellow gives a green. This is termed a subtractive mixture.

But when the two colors are mixed as colored lights thrown on a screen or, what comes to the same thing, as small colored dots placed side by side and seen from far enough away so that their images blur in the observer's eye, a quite different effect is produced. Here the mixture is called "additive." For the color of such a mixture is the result of the addition of all the color components of each of the colored lights, or spots, in question. Since yellow contains yellow, red and green, and blue contains blue, green and violet, the mixture of yellow and blue lights will give, not green alone, but all the colors together. Since white light is a mixture of all the colors, a blue light plus a yellow light gives white. And the result of a speckling of spots of blue and yellow, if the spots are of an equal darkness, will give a luminous gray. In the same way, the mixture of green and violet paint will give dull blue, but mixed as lights or spots they give a neutral tone. Blue and orange paint give gray. But blue and orange spots will give dull pink. As one can see, the result of a color mixture depends on whether the paints are mixed beforehand on the palette, or put down as spots side by side on the canvas, and mixed only by the blurring of the spectator's eye.

To the Impressionists, all this was new and extremely valuable, and it was by using this theory of the additive mixtures that the Impressionists, with all their brightest colors, painted their gray pictures. But these pictures were of a completely new and glittering sort of gray.

The theory of the additive and subtractive varieties of color mixing still stands uncontested today. But the part of the nineteenth century color theory having to do with the classification of colors is now discredited. The notions held about the structure of color were much too simple. The physicists considered that the color of a substance is given by the predominance of one particular wave length in the light which it reflects. They decided, as a consequence, that any color tone can be classified and reproduced if three facts about it are known: first its value, or the total amount of light it reflects, measured on a scale going from black carbon to white paper; second its hue, or its exact position on a spectrum band ranging from red through yellow to violet—in other words, the color's name; and third, its intensity, or the color's purity, measured on a scale ranging from neutral gray to full color strength. Each of these facts can be given as a number. So that if three numbers were determined, it was supposed that any color tone could be found, identified and matched. In fact there was published at enormous expense by a German named Ostwald, an exhaustive atlas of color, a color dictionary which followed this system, and which was supposed to contain samples in actual tone of every possible color.

This sounds pretty, complete and convincing. Unfortunately it does not work. There is no such simple correspondence between the color of an object and an exact position on the spectrum band. Giving a color's name by no means gives a wave-length number. Although 0.656279μ denotes the position of a red line in the spectrum, the color of a red object is not so neat a parcel, nor can it be reduced to a simple location on any scale. What the eye perceives as red is a very complicated affair indeed, and this one flaw invalidates the whole system of classification.

The system has still another flaw. What we now know to be accidental characteristics of the pigments we have, these theorists took to be the essential characteristics of color itself. In this respect the system is as mistaken and arbitrary as the eighteenth century system of the three primaries. We, today, accustomed to the practices of color photography, know that any three reasonably different colors can be taken as primaries—red, blue-green and violet, or red-violet, blue and green, or any other convenient triad. The eighteenth century believed that red, yellow and blue were the only true primary colors, simply because of the accident that the brightest colors they possessed were carmine, gamboge and ultramarine blue. The nineteenth and early twentieth century theorists were misled in exactly the same way. The Munsell color tree, and later Arthur Pope's color solid—two of the principal systems of color classification—considered that purple is a naturally dark color and placed it at a low value level, almost at black; and considered yellow to be a naturally light color and put its natural value almost at white. We, on the other hand, now know that it is chiefly by accident that our yellows are light and our purples dark. Purple is dark only because most of the purple colors we have are got by a subtractive mixture of red and blue paint and consequently reflect very little light. And the bright yellows we have are light in tone because our yellow pigments reflect not only the yellow light but all the red and green as well—in fact all the visible spectrum except the blue. If we had a pigment which reflected only the yellow part of the spectrum, it would seem so dark as to appear a sort of brown. Mixed with blue it would give black instead of green. And a purple pigment which reflected red and blue as efficiently as pale cadmium yellow reflects the red and green, would be very light indeed, and this despite the fact that the eye's greatest sensitivity lies in the range of yellow-green, not in the blues and reds.

Thus, contrary to what the nineteenth century supposed, the brightness of the color of a substance depends very little on the preponderance of one color vibration, of one spectrum line, in the light it reflects. If this were so, there would be no purple color at all, for there is no spectrum line or wave length of light corresponding to the color we know as purple. The violet of the rainbow's VIBGYOR (shorthand for Violet, Indigo, Blue, Green, Yellow, Orange, Red—the spectrum colors in their natural order) is at most a purplish blue, scarcely more purple than ultramarine. What we call purple is the sensation we receive when our eye sees red and blue light at the same time.

Nowadays we have reason to believe that the intensity of the color sensation our eye receives depends uniquely on the absence, in the color, of the color's complement. Pale cadmium appears an intense yellow because it reflects everything in the visible spectrum except the complement of yellow, which is blue. A red pigment of greatest possible intensity would reflect all of the spectrum's blue and red and yellow, but none of the green, and would be exactly such a red as is found in certain flowers, petunias, zinnias and others, which with all the paints the painter has today he still cannot match. The intensest green would have none of the violet red or purple blue, but would reflect all the rest of the spectrum range from blue-green through red-orange.

Herein lies one of the reasons why painters have such trouble with green. Green leaves in nature reflect a certain amount of red and orange. This red the painter cannot supply to his green paint without dulling its intensity. Seeing, nevertheless, that the color of the leaves is bright, the painter tries to represent its brightness by using his brightest green paint, with the painful result which we all well know, that most green trees in painting look like spinach.

So that color turns out to be a more complicated entity than it was formerly supposed. We are now aware that a color, such as a red, can appear to be a quite bright red without having any specific red in it at all, if it reflects violet-red and red-orange. Two colors can be made up, composed of different pigments, which appear to match exactly. But if the light is changed, they will no longer match, and they will also probably have quite a different effect in color mixtures. Each pigment has its own characteristic spectrum curve, which can be drawn by a machine that records how much light the pigment reflects at each point on the spectrum band. This curve is so unmistakable that in the recorded spectrum curve of a mixture of pigments, each pigment can be identified by the presence of its characteristic curve, and its proportion in the mixture calculated. In sum, each pigment has its own individual character. Replacing one pigment by a similar one in a color mixture generally produces a quite different quality —like replacing a flute by a clarinet in an orchestral chord. Which, of course, the painters have known all the while.

This comparison of a pigment to an instrument of the orchestra is the only analogy I know to be found between the arts of music and painting, or at any rate between the musician's sounds and the painter's colors. The nineteenth and early twentieth century color theorists, knowing that monochromatic light has a definite rate of vibration, attempted to identify this vibration number with musical pitch. Denman Ross, professor at Harvard and an able painter, thought to establish a color keyboard which would correspond to the keyboard of a piano. The painter was to lay out on his palette a series of preestablished color tones, which he would then play, like a musical instrument, either in single notes or mixed as chords.

Denman Ross's own pictures, painted with his scaled palettes, have great charm and even great charm of color. But no one, as far as I know, except the inventor himself, was ever able to derive any advantage from these preestablished palettes or, in using them, to paint with any but the most monotonous effects. The trouble with the system, of course, is that the painter does not paint with pure color. He has nothing to do with simple combinations of monochromatic light. He paints with pigments. These pigments are in no respect pure colors. They are material substances which already reflect very complicated chords of colored light. The qualities they possess are by no means uniform. They can be graded, as lighter or darker, warmer or colder, or brighter or duller. But there is no way of placing them in a uniform or equally spaced row. And even if it could be done, the painter would gain nothing by it. To fix these diverse substances on an established scale would be as arbitrary, as limiting and as useless, as the taste piano in Huysmans' *A Rebours*, where striking a note on the keyboard lets glide into the operator's mouth a single drop each of a different cordial, of absinthe, benedictine, cointreau, scotch or gin, to form a gustatory music.

To mistake a shade of paint for a note of music is just as absurd as this. The only comparison between paint and sound which is not completely misleading is the analogy of a pigment to a musical instrument. This, limited as it is, does describe the way a painter makes use of his pigments' possibilities. In fact, a treatise not unlike a treatise on orchestration could be written on the painter's pigments: how the transparent colors, alizarin crimson and viridian, have one effect when used transparently, and give a different effect and color when mixed with white; how burnt sienna, ugly and hot alone, can be turned by the admixture of Prussian or ultramarine blue into an unending series of useful browns and grays; how Venetian red and cobalt violet, in spite of their being lively and beautiful colors, seem almost impossible to find a use for, although Venetian red appears with great splendor in the pictures of Tiepolo, and much of Bonnard's work is based on the successful combination of cobalt violet and cadmium orange, another difficult color; how black alone with white will make a sort of dirty lilac, not a gray. All this is very like the composer's knowing that a horn has different qualities of tone in different registers or how to make audible a pizzicato cello passage by underlining it with inaudible short notes on the trombone.

Firsthand knowledge such as this about materials is very useful to the painter. But no one any longer believes that beautiful color can be got by following some color scale or by observing some mathematical system. On the other hand, the ordinary painter's idea that color is something which is obtained by mixing paints together has serious scientific support. But even this is less secure than the painter thinks. A new theory of color mixing has recently been developed which will upset all the painter's practices and notions about color. It is also likely to knock his established palette of reasonably permanent pigments sky-high. This bombshell is Dr. Herbert Ives' system of the subtractive mixture of the minus colors.

Dr. Ives bases his system on the possibility of finding three pigments, each of which will reflect exactly two thirds and no more of the visible spectrum. The third of the spectrum each pigment lacks must in each case be different. Thus, the first of these pigments must reflect all the red and green but none of the blue; the next all the blue and green but none of the red; and the third, all the red and blue but none of the green. These pigments are called the minus colors, each named after that part of the spectrum it does not reflect. Minus blue, reflecting red and green, would of course appear yellow. Minus red, reflecting green and blue, would be a peacock blue. Minus green, reflecting red and blue, a mauve. Dr. Ives maintains that if a set of three perfect minus color pigments of this description could be found, mixing these three paints would give all colors. Two of them together would give the bright colors at their highest intensity, and the mixture of all three would give the muted tones.

If one mixed, for example, the minus blue paint, which reflects only red and green, with the minus green, reflecting only red and blue, the green and blue components of the light reflected would be canceled out. Consequently the resulting color would be a pure red. The color quality of the red, whether toward the orange or the purple, would depend on which of the two minus colors predominated in the mixture. If to this mixture the minus red were also added, the red itself would be canceled out and the resulting mixture would appear black.

All this sounds not very different from the old theory of the three primaries. But there is more to follow. It appears that a more satisfactory system which would produce even brighter colors could be arrived at if it were possible to find a more numerous set of minus primaries. Let us imagine a set of seven. Here again, each pigment of the set must reflect all the spectrum band except one small sector. But in this case each of the gaps must lie in one of the sections of the spectrum indicated by a single letter of the word VIBGYOR, our name for the rainbow colors in their proper order. Each one of these minus pigments would have as color a slightly different purplish gray, almost a white. Nevertheless, the mixture of these grays, an endless series of the most brilliant and varied colors, unobtainable today, could be made. For example, the combination of the minus violet, the minus indigo and the minus blue (of—VIB, so to speak) would remove all the blue-violet side of the spectrum and produce an intense yellow. The combination of minus yellow, minus orange and minus red, of—YOR, would give the brightest possible blue. The mixture of all the minus pigments except one, say for example, the minus red, by removing from the light reflected by the mixture all color save a narrow band in the red, would give a limited, but pure, red tone. All the pigments mixed together would, of course, give black.

Working on the simpler problem of the set of three minus colors, Dr. Ives has found that pale cadmium yellow is perfectly satisfactory as a minus blue; thalo blue or Chinese blue are both fairly good minus reds, and the mauve colored phospho-molybdo-tungstic acid lake of rhodamine 6o (one of the printers' ink colors which according to Dr. Ives is quite as safe as alizarin) serves reasonably well as a minus green. Working with only these three pigments and white, Dr. Ives, who besides being a physicist is a painter of taste and talent as well, has produced pictures of extraordinary brightness of color. What is more surprising and convincing, the pictures he has painted with these limited means exhibit a great variety of color schemes, a thing impossible in any other three-color painting system I have ever heard of.

These three pigments, Dr. Ives informs me, are not the perfect ones for his purpose. The absorption bands of the minus green and minus blue (of the cadmium yellow and of the violet-red lake) do not fit exactly enough to exclude all the green and blue, and as a consequence the red got by their mixture is not perfectly pure and bright. But even though these pigments may be imperfect, the system works astonishingly well. If three perfectly fitted minus pigments could be found, and there is no reason to suppose they will not be, they will be of extraordinary interest to the painter.

Of even greater interest would be the finding of a set of the seven minus primaries. Both painting and color would then become completely different from anything we know today. With the pigments we now possess, variety of color quality can be obtained only in the degraded tones. Bright colors like vermilion or cobalt, if they are to be bright, must of necessity be only what they are. If they are to appear on the painter's canvas as bright colors, they must be there as themselves, in their own character and unmistakable. A bright red can be got only with vermilion, or with white covered with a transparent coat of alizarin crimson. A bright blue is pure cobalt or ultramarine, a bright yellow, pure cadmium. Any mixture of another color, like a touch of vermilion in the alizarin to vary its color quality, invariably degrades its hue and contaminates its brilliance. But with the seven minus primaries, the minus V, I, G, B, Y, O, R's at his disposal, the painter would have access to as great a variety in the character of his brightest colors, as many ways of producing bright tones of the same hue but of completely different character, as he has now in producing variety in his browns and beiges. For example, the combination —I, —G, and —B, with the addition of varying amounts of three of the remaining four minus primaries, would give an endless number of the brightest reds, as different in quality and as numerous as the reds to be seen in a bed of zinnias.

But whether the painter himself will like these pigments, once they are found, is not so certain. The color practices he uses today are based on the pigments he has painfully learned can be depended on. The theory of the minus colors will force him on to the use of new and untried materials. The permanence of these new pigments will certainly satisfy the ordinary commercial standards. That is to say they will undoubtedly be permanent enough to last the lifetime of an automobile; otherwise they will not be put on the market. But whether they will be permanent enough to last the lifetime of a painter's fame is another matter. When these pigments are found, which I am convinced will be fairly soon, the painter will be forced to face all over again the question that has so perplexed and bedeviled painters of the last hundred years: How long will my picture last?

CHAPTER EIGHT

MUMMY, MAUVE AND ORPIMENT

It is therefore that we ourselves, though quite enamoured of experiment, have never felt the least desire to assay this pigment (mummy), seeing nothing to be gained by smearing our canvas with part perhaps of the wife of Potiphar, that might not be as easily secured by materials less frail and of more sober character. . . .
However there is this to add in order to say all: viz, that the student *can* obtain genuine Egyptian mummy at our color shops, but he cannot purchase real Arabian asphaltum.

From *A Handbook of Oil Painting*, by "An American Artist" [Laughton Osborn], Edition of 1865.

No one except a painter or a museum curator ever understands how fragile a picture is. To other people a picture is a safe, stable, solid object, quite as immutable as money or truth, Shakespeare's plays or Leonardo's *Last Supper*, or any other generally admired idea. But the painter who makes pictures and the curator who protects them know that the *Last Supper*, as a painting by the hand of Leonardo, has not been in existence for more than three hundred years. The fabric of the picture has been many times destroyed and reconstituted. And all that now remains of its original existence is our idea of it. As an idea in the mind, the *Last Supper* possesses the relative permanence of other things inside the mind. As a picture by the hand of Leonardo, it has long ago yielded to the flux and decay to which all things outside the mind are subject.

Of this flux of nature the painter is painfully aware. His flowers fade before he gets them on his canvas. Dust settles on his still-life objects and his peaches rot. His models fail to come and on no two days does the weather on his landscape stay the same. Style in costume changes, wars come and go, and cities rise and fall. Out of this bustle and movement and hurry and disintegration he desperately labors to extract some small permanence, some minor stability; only to find, as he must, that the few square feet of relative immortality he has devised for the world he sees and delights in, these pictures he has made, are also part of the outside world, and like it also subject to decay. And a painter, wandering through a museum, peering into the dark corners of the paintings, searching out the signs of mortality in the masterpieces of the past, the cracks and patches, spoiled colors, repaintings and overcleanings, can become very unhappy indeed. Here a color has faded. Here is the scar where a hole has been mended—perhaps a screwdriver slipped when the packing case was opened. These are the ridges left where the canvas has once been folded back to fit a smaller frame. Here is a spot of repaint that has darkened, or a mouth grown vague, chapped by some restorer's solvents.

Markings such as these in the older pictures do not surprise the painter or even overly distress him. Accidents, after all, are part of the vicissitudes of a long life. It seems proper that a Ryder should be cracked and a Whistler black—he has never seen them otherwise. But put him in front of some recent picture which has gone bad—say the George Bellows portrait of an old man which now hangs in the Metropolitan—and he will not like it at all. These pasty colors, this disintegrating and darkened paint, in a picture which only a short time ago was witty and alive, are not pleasant for him to contemplate. This is perhaps the fate that awaits his own pictures. And do what he will, it is only by luck or election that they will escape it.

It is not accident the painter fears, but his own lack of knowledge. The older pictures have lasted until now because they were solidly constructed. Their painters had access to a body of systematic knowledge about painting methods and materials. But today, knowledge about paints and painting is scattered and untested. Much knowledge that was once the common property of all painters is now irretrievably lost. The life of a new-made picture is endangered by vices of construction that no one, no one at all, can be certain he knows how to avoid. And although we have magnificent new pigments the older painters did not possess, we no longer have any certain or tested knowledge about the paint we make from them, or how long it will last in our pictures.

There is in the Frick Collection a portrait of a Lady Clanbrassil in a blue dress, painted by Van Dyke in 1636. Near enough to make comparing easy is a Renoir of a mother and two children, painted in 1874, the year of the first Impressionist exhibition. The Van Dyke is fresh and bright. Beside it, the Renoir, painted scarcely seventy-five years ago, looks sad and faded. Renoir's reputation rests to a large extent on the fire and clarity of his colors. Certainly many of his pictures are as bright today as on the day they were painted. But the colors in this particular picture seem to have suffered considerable changes. The mother and her children stand beside what appears to have once been a bed of flowers. Whatever reds the flowers may once have had are now gone. The reds in the flesh tones, if there were ever any, seem to have disappeared as well, all save the vermilion carnation of the lips and cheeks. The violet of the mother's dress is dull and muddy, and the dress of the doll one of the children carries, though it still has some of the characteristic tone of artificial ultramarine blue, has turned almost to black. Compared to these now tentative and wistful colors, the Van Dyke glows like some huge lump of clear blue glass.

Nevertheless it is quite possible that Van Dyke's blue was painted with what we would now consider a bad or fugitive color, like smalt or azurite or even indigo. It could not have been Prussian blue, which was not in use until the eighteenth century, nor cobalt either, for that was not invented until the nineteenth. Most probably, however, the blue is real ultramarine; though this mineral was, I believe, particularly hard to obtain at the time this picture was painted. Besides, Van Dyke's blue seems to have a more greenish tinge than real ultramarine usually shows. But whatever the pigment may be, whether ultramarine, indigo, smalt or azurite, it is, after more than three hundred years, still brighter than the blue in Renoir's picture. Renoir's blue, unquestionably our artificial form of ultramarine, a pigment we consider to be perfectly dependable, has changed; other of his colors have faded as well. Something must be wrong. Either the bright new pigments of the Impressionists were not as stable as we imagined them to be, or the painting methods of the seventeenth century were more dependable than our own.

The pigments employed by the seventeenth and eighteenth century painters were certainly not what we ourselves would consider the most satisfactory or reliable. Their palette was quite limited. Its basis was white lead and the earth colors got from various colored clays. For good, bright reds there were vermilion—considered today unreliable—and the transparent reds made from dyestuffs like madder and grain. The word "grain" we now only know in the expression "dyed in grain." This does not mean, as the dictionaries would have it, dyed in the yarn before weaving. It means quite simply dyed red with grain—with grana or kermes, a little red bug like the cochineal insect.

For blues, besides real ultramarine, there were azurite, another blue mineral stone; smalt, a pulverized pottery glaze tinted with copper, coarse grained, weak and said to work badly in oil; and indigo, a vegetable dye with a miserable reputation for permanence. After the first quarter of the eighteenth century there was Prussian.

They had almost no good green pigments at all. Green earth was the best, and that is both dull and weak. There were the unstable vegetable greens like sap green and iris green. A number of copper greens were to be had, all of them dangerous and fugitive save one made by some process of boiling verdigris in a resin. It was applied as a glaze between layers of varnish which served to seal the pigment from the air. Used in this way verdigris was sometimes satisfactory. It is this verdigris resin which was the celebrated green of Veronese; it has no connection with the green which bears his name today. The green robe in Veronese's *Choice of Hercules*, and the green background of Bronzino's extremely elegant young man, both in the Frick Collection, were probably painted with this doubtful concoction. If not carefully prepared and even more carefully employed, this green was likely to turn brown. I have always supposed that it was precisely the degeneration of this green in the landscapes of the old masters which set the otherwise unaccountable fashion for the brown trees, so affected by the Romantic painters.

In the yellow pigments there was equal difficulty. Yellow ocher, which is dull, and Naples yellow, which has little tinting strength, were the only safe ones. There was orpiment (auripigmentum, or gold color), an arsenic yellow, extremely poisonous, fugitive and destructive to all other colors unless used with great care; king's yellow, a sort of burned white lead; Indian yellow, made from the urine of camels fed on mango leaves, a pigment I believe no longer available; and gamboge, from Cambodia, a dye and a violent cathartic, but as a pigment unreliable. There were no bright violets or purples at all.

With all these lacks, restrictions and difficulties, the painters seem to have managed quite well, and some of the most questionable pigments they used—saffron, I am told, among them—remain undamaged in their pictures today because they had some reliable methods for protecting them. Their painting methods, if not their pigments, could be depended upon. The painter knew what he was doing and what he was working with. His information, originally collected by the guilds, remained for the most part reliable well after the end of the eighteenth century. *A Painter's Handbook* of 1821 recommends a list of colors which our present-day restorers and laboratory technicians would find in no way objectionable.

With the development of chemistry in the nineteenth century, all this was changed. A host of new pigments were invented, some good and some worthless. The guilds no longer existed. The painting academies were not equipped to collect information about the new pigments and help the painter find out which he might safely use. The color merchants themselves were equally unhelpful. Already in 1801, in an English color merchant's catalogue, *A Treatise on Ackerman's Superfine Watercolors, With Directions How to Prepare and Use them,* one finds such substances as carmine, burnt carmine, calcined vitriol, and gall stone, all so unreliable that their very names have been carefully forgotten, and yet these pigments are listed indiscriminately among the tried and standard colors. Nor is there any indication whatsoever of the impermanence of this merchandise. The preamble to the catalogue boasts that these were the colors supplied to Turner. If it can be believed that Turner was influenced in his choice of pigments by Ackerman's encomiums, it is no mystery why certain of Turner's pictures have faded.

That many of Turner's pictures have changed color cannot be denied. There is one in the Frick Collection which is without doubt not at all as Turner left it. It is a picture of the Cologne-Dusseldorf ferry pulling into dock. The shadow tones of the boat and the darks in the foreground are today a hot and heavy orange-red, completely out of key with the cool tones of the sky and background. Their color is that of unmixed burnt sienna. It was a common practice of the eighteenth and nineteenth century painters, and probably of Turner as well, to make shadow tones with a mixture of burnt sienna and Prussian blue. These pigments, with the addition of white, give a wide and useful range of neutral browns and grays. If, in place of the dependable Prussian blue in the mixture, Turner had been persuaded to use a fugitive indigo or one of Ackerman's undependable new blues, the subsequent disappearance of the blue from the shadow tones would account for the red-orange appearance the picture has today.

These new untested colors, when they began to appear, had all the prestige of modernity. No one, I am sure, believed them to be as unreliable as they later proved. How bad many of them were can be judged from the fabrics of the time. For it was as dyes for fabrics that the bright new colors found their widest and most legitimate employment.

Before the nineteenth century fabric dyes had been reasonably fast. This can be seen in any museum where there is a collection of tapestries. Even today there is no more beautiful red in existence than the red in the background of the famous *Lady and the Unicorn* which has lasted since the sixteenth century. On the other hand, few of the nineteenth century tapestries have kept their original tones. All seem to have changed to moldy browns and olives. The fragility of the nineteenth century fabric dyes is even more dramatically demonstrated in the series of inaugural gowns of the wives of the presidents on display at the Smithsonian Institute. All those after Dolly Madison's of 1809 have lost their color. Mrs. Coolidge's is probably the one nearest to its original hue—something like the color of a fresh shrimp paste. But Mrs. Harding's retains only the faintest hint of aquamarine, and Mrs. Roosevelt's is only a whisper of pink. The rest have no longer any color at all.

Most of this fading is the fault of the now notorious aniline dyes. But long before these were found fabric colors had become undependable. Mrs. Monroe's gown, of 1815, forty years before the anilines were known, is as faded as any of the others in the collection. The reason lies in the great industrial expansion of the early nineteenth century. More textiles were being manufactured than ever before and there was not enough of the old, standard dyestuffs to satisfy the demand. Manufacturers began to try substitutes, adulterants and new inventions, few of them satisfactory. When the coal tar dyes were at length discovered, they quickly replaced all others, for they were strongest, brightest and cheapest. Their colors were the most modern. They had only one disadvantage, and that, for the trade, a minor one: few of them were stable or even light-proof.

Mauve, the first of the anilines, was discovered in 1856, only eighteen years before the first Impressionist exposition, and mauve was immediately followed by innumerable others. These anilines, synthesized from coal, rainbow colors produced by a miracle of science from black tar, were the most astounding achievement of the new organic chemistry. They were at once made into lakes and turned over to the painters.

The word "lake" does not indicate a particular color. A lake can be red, green or even black. A lake is simply a dye made into a paint. A dye has no body and consequently is not a pigment; it is a soluble stain. Untreated, it cannot be used for making paint. It would stain the brushes, paper or canvas, dissolve in adjacent patches of paint and "bleed through" any number of coats put on to cover it—as amateur house painters frequently discover to their sorrow when they attempt to put paint over figured wallpaper. A lake is an insoluble and more or less transparent base which has been dyed with the dye in question. Thus the dye is fixed, given body and can be made into paint. The process itself has been known since the earliest times. There was nothing new about the nineteenth century lakes except the dyes from which they were made. The only difficulty was that few of the dyes had any permanence whatsoever. It was the doubtful aniline lakes and other equally questionable new pigments which formed the largest part of the new colors made available to the painters.

Stable or not, the new colors had beautiful names. And the painters of the 60's, 70's and 80's were presented with increasingly varied, tempting and exciting color lists which, pure poetry though they be, carried no indication of the colors' relative stability. As an example of the luxuriance of these catalogues, let me quote from a list of colors offered in 1876—at the height of the Impressionist expansion—by the American firm of Devoe. Here, as in all these catalogues, the colors we now consider reliable are lost among and vastly outnumbered by the colors which we have learned to know as fugitive and dangerous such as these:

Beginning with the reds, Devoe lists brown red, burnt carmine, burnt lake, carmine numbers 6, 8, 40, 40 nacarat and oriental; carmine lake super, extra, fine and A, B, C and D; Chatamuc lake, extract of vermilion, Florentine lake, geranium lake, imitation carmine, and the lakes of mahogany, magenta, maroon, mauve and Munich; Persian red, purple of Cassius [which may be stable; it is a salt of gold], pure scarlet [this is mercuric iodide, the most brilliant and the most transitory of all the colors], rose lake and royal purple, Turkey red, Tuscan red, Van Dyke red, and Solferino, violet, Vienna and Victoria lakes.

Among the blues are Bremen blue, indigo and intense blue, Monthier's blue [which I cannot identify], and steel and turnasol blue. The greens begin with chromate of arsenic and continue with chrome green, emerald green, green lake, Milori's green, olive green [a mixture of indigo and Indian yellow], green bice, Paul Veronese green, Scheele's green [all copper compounds and unstable], sap green, Verona green, Victoria green, Zinzobar green and verdigris (crystallized). For yellows there are gamboge, Dutch pink, Robert's lake from number 1 to 8, gaude lake, imperial orange, king's yellow, Milori yellow, patent yellow, perfect yellow, platina yellow, orpiment yellow, orpiment red, turbith mineral, and yellow madder. Among the browns are asphaltum (Arabian), bitumen (French) and mummy (Egyptian), listed at only eight dollars a pound.

Many colors in these lists may have been fugitive; these browns were actually destructive. They were the principal cause of the pall of Egyptian darkness that now covers so many of the nineteenth century pictures.

Brown was the favorite color of the Romantic painters, the color of the golden tone of age, of comfortable warmth, of poetic mystery and darkness. The most romantic brown of all could be got with asphaltum, bitumen, or the ground-up fragments of an Egyptian mummy. Not that these substances could be transformed into anything that might properly be called paint. Ground in a painting medium they dissolved in it and became a sort of tar—rich, cool, deep, transparent, completely satisfying to the Romantic tastes, and completely incapable of drying. Spread on a canvas in anything but the thinnest of final glazes, this tar ran in hot weather, contracted in cold, gathered in drops, dripped, cracked, and disrupted any color painted beneath it or on top of it. I have been told of an otherwise handsome nineteenth century portrait whose eyes, painted in asphaltum, ran down on to the cheeks after an especially hot day. The great broad crevices and the alligator skin one finds in the dark passages of so many of the paintings of the time (like the cracks in the pictures of Ryder) are the almost certain signs of the presence of asphaltum, bitumen, or the dust of a mummified Pharaoh.

Another destructive agent, sugar of lead, a dryer, is listed in all these catalogues. Bitumen, asphaltum and mummy tars require great doses of these dryers if they are to harden at all, and such dryers have the worst possible effect on the durability of a paint film. For they shorten not only the time it takes a paint to dry, but by speeding up the whole process of its oxidation, shorten also the time the paint will take to fall at length to dust. Dryers were needed as well for all the aniline lakes the painter now employed and for the new zinc white which was coming into fashion.

Before the nineteenth century the standard painter's white had always been white lead. But by the middle of the nineteenth century zinc white was beginning to replace it. Zinc white (zinc oxide) has a certain use as a mild antiseptic. Ground in cold cream it finds considerable employment on the beaches of the Los Angeles region in protecting the noses of actors and athletes from an excess of sun. But ground in linseed oil and made into paint, it has almost nothing to recommend it. It dries badly to a brittle paint film. It has little covering power. In coats thick enough to cover it is quite likely to crack. White lead, on the other hand, the standard white of all the older painters, is a dense, opaque pigment. It has splendid covering power and dries quickly to a tough and flexible paint film. It is, of course, a dangerous poison, even more dangerous because its effects are cumulative. The painter using it must be careful about smoking as he paints. Even the tiniest bit absorbed may eventually have very disagreeable consequences. This has never stopped its use as a cosmetic and it has been employed by women until very recently indeed to cover blemishes and whiten the complexion. In fact, one of the practical jokes for dinner parties described by Giovanni Battista della Porta, the seventeenth century playwright and physicist in his book on *Natural Magic*, takes advantage of this use of the substance. Along with how to make an egg as big as a hundred eggs, how to serve up ducklings roasted but still quacking, and how to drive away unwelcome guests by scattering the joint with small sections of gut lute string, which with the heat will squirm and look like maggots, Della Porta tells how, by burning sulphur under the table, to make the white lead on the ladies' faces turn black.

As a pigment, however, white lead has a more legitimate, and certainly less dangerous use than as a cosmetic. And, since Roman times and no one knows how long before, white lead has been the only white employed by painters in either oil or tempera. In the second half of the nineteenth century, however, white lead began to be replaced by zinc white on the oil painter's palette, and for a very curious reason. It was that white lead, when used in water color, is known to blacken.

This effect, of course, is common and well known. But when white lead is made into paint by being ground in egg or oil or varnish, it is quite sufficiently protected, and I myself have never seen an oil painting in which the white lead has spoiled. Yet white lead was attacked on this ground, and, once its reputation began to go, blackening was not the only thing held against it. It was blamed for the faults of all the other colors as well. If indigo, or carmine, or mauve faded, it was because white lead had eaten it up. If verdigris, or Scheele's green or green verditer or mountain blue or any of the other unstable copper colors changed, it was held to be because of their mixture with white lead. If orpiment misbehaved, it was because it had become contaminated. When king's yellow and minium—the red lead used for painting bridges—tarnished, it was not because they were unstable colors in themselves; they were thought unstable because they were lead compounds. That old stand-by, Naples yellow, made of lead and antimony, the one reliable yellow the old masters had, was discarded. Some fictitious pigment, some mineral supposed to have been formerly mined near Naples and now no longer available, was imagined to account for the presence and the permanence of what was obviously Naples yellow in the pictures of the old masters. For the few painters who still insisted on it, the color merchants prepared an imitation out of ocher and cadmium yellow. It was not until well after the first quarter of our century, when white lead began to come back into fashion, that the use of Naples yellow was resumed.

But these are minor controversies. Reputable or not, zinc white and Naples yellow are still the best of pigments when compared to other substances of these nineteenth century color lists, to mauve, carmine, pure scarlet, verdigris and mummy. The real difficulty about all these colors was that they were all unclassified. No one knew for certain which of them to avoid. The color merchants' catalogues placed the most untrustworthy of the new inventions impartially alongside the standard tested pigments, and made no discrimination whatsoever among them. These color lists also contained the new pigments which we have come to consider reliable, like viridian, cobalt blue, alizarin crimson and the cadmium yellows and oranges. But none of the catalogues made any attempt to grade this merchandise according to its stability. Painters, as always, wrote manuals, which, like the manuals of today, exhibited a remarkable diversity of opinion. One would recommend and another discourage the use of "impastoes," "gumptions," and "megilps"—pasty painting mediums, buttery mixtures of mastic varnish and drying oil, supposed to have been invented by a painter named MacGulip. Another described a painting ground made of calcined bones spread upon a bare canvas with common paste, or recommended for use in water-color saffron, turmeric, zedoary (a spice root like ginger) and "Spanish juice, or extract of licorice"—all, I am certain, more suitable in pickles than in paints. It is astonishing that of the pictures painted with unknown colors and with such strange advice anything should be left at all.

The answer is that the pictures still remaining were not painted like this. Painters, in general, are fairly sensible men. Even in Romantic times they employed the fine poetic fury only when necessary to impress a client; almost never for selecting painting materials. Yet, it was from these untested and unqualified lists that the nineteenth century painters had to choose their paints. They escaped from the bitumens and brown sauces of the 40's and 50's only to find themselves beset by the anilines of the 70's and 80's, and it was with these almost untried new bright colors that the Impressionist pictures were painted.

It would not be surprising if many of the Impressionist pictures were less solid than we once supposed. Vincent Van Gogh wrote to his brother Theo from Arles in 1890: "All the colors that the Impressionists have brought into fashion are unstable. So there is all the more reason to use them boldly . . . time will tone them down only too well." It is sad but true. It is, of course, difficult to find out which particular colors any one of these painters did or did not employ. But Van Gogh himself writes of using emerald and malachite greens (unstable copper salts), geranium lake (a fugitive aniline), orange lead (like the red lead used to protect ironwork, by no means a solid color) and three tones of chrome yellow. The yellows in his famous Sunflowers are chrome, and undoubtedly were once cruder and brighter than their now subdued and harmonious gold. The changes in Van Gogh's other pictures have not been all as fortunate. Changes of color and value render passages in certain of the pictures difficult to read. The billiard table in his well-known *Night Café* was once bright green. In fact Van Gogh calls it green in one of his letters. It is now tan, with no trace of green whatever. Mr. Murray Pease, restorer at the Metropolitan Museum, described in the *Art News* of November 1948 the state of one of Van Gogh's Cypress series which he had examined. According to Mr. Pease, the paint on this picture is not yet dry. The surface can still be dented with a fingernail, and is still soluble in turpentine and even water. The Lord only knows what Van Gogh used to paint it with. Perhaps a shipment of colors from Theo had been delayed, and he was using oil colors bought from the local house painters' supply shop.

Other Impressionists were perhaps more careful—or more fortunate—in their choice of pigments. But all their pictures are subject to another danger—that of varnish.

Pictures when they are finished are usually allowed to dry a year and then are varnished. The varnish brightens the colors, darkens the shadows which have lightened in drying, equalizes the surface by giving the picture an equal gloss. Most important of all, the varnish protects the picture from the dirt which would otherwise collect in the cracks of the paint where it is impossible to remove it. But a coat of varnish is not very durable. Its life is seldom more than fifty years. A varnish may turn yellow, or it may bloom and develop bluish, chalky spots like bloom on grapes, or become opaque or black or dirty or simply turn to dust and disappear. Whenever a picture is cleaned, which is the commonest job a restorer is called upon to do, the cleaning is accomplished by removing the old varnish and replacing it by a fresh one.

Nowadays pictures need more frequent cleanings than before. The air of our cities contains sulphurous acid, from the burning of the sulphur in coal. This acid erodes not only buildings and statues exposed to the rains, but also pictures indoors as well. Any picture of any value over a certain age is sure to have been submitted to restorers for cleaning several times.

The Impressionists' pictures are more frequently in need of cleaning than the old masters'. Most were painted in clear light colors with blue and lavender shadows. These clear light tones and bright cool shadows, so different from the warm shadows of the older pictures, are soiled and degraded by even the slightest yellowing of the varnish, a yellowing which on a darker or a warmer picture would not be noticed at all. And on account of the softness of the commercially manufactured paint used, the removal of spoiled varnish is a delicate job, one that is much more dangerous and uncertain than the removal of a varnish from the tough paint surface of an old master.

For this reason, Impressionist pictures are generally varnished with a soft, thin, spirit varnish which, when it yellows, can easily be removed. With Cézanne, this is not always the case; a yellow varnish on a Cézanne has sometimes other values and considerations. Cézanne's reputation as a painter and his personal legend as well have for some time been rapidly growing, and by now have become almost comparable to Rembrandt's. Today the comparison is frequently underlined and made more evident by the application to his pictures of a Rembrandt varnish, heavy, glassy, rich and amber. Equipped with such a surface, a picture by Cézanne can look plutocratic and ancestral enough to satisfy the most Rembrandt-minded picture collector. In other respects, however, the results of such a varnish are perhaps less fortunate. Cézanne's colors are seldom as pale and delicate and susceptible to the film of a dirty varnish as are, for example, Monet's. Nevertheless, the central framework of his color composition is most frequently a balance of the oranges and blues. The orange-yellow of the Rembrandt-type varnish turns Cézanne's blues to grays, upsets his color composition, and falsifies the picture's character. On account of the thin paint film so many of these paintings possess, a hard varnish such as this will always be difficult to remove without doing grave injury.

Many of the Cézannes have just as thick a paint and rough a surface as the other Impressionists. With a rough impasto surface of this sort, it is almost impossible to remove a spoiled varnish from the crevices of the paint without overcleaning and "skinning" the crests of the ridges. When the canvas of such a picture must be repaired or replaced, as often happens, the restorer has first to take a cast of the surface of the picture, so that when the picture is ironed onto its new canvas backing, the paint ridges, supported in the cast, will not be flattened out—a difficult job, and one not always undertaken. Besides, the paint used in these pictures is soft. It was a paint which was, for the most part, manufactured in commercial quantities, by makers who were sometimes none too scrupulous, ground in slow drying oils and with all sorts of adulterants, waxes and non-drying substances added to keep it from drying in the tube before it could be sold. Pictures painted with such paint can never become really firm or resistant to solvents and cleaning fluids. Their care and preservation will always present a difficult problem to restorers.

There is little difference between the paint of the Impressionists and the commercial tube colors in use today. Nor will the restorers of the future find the pictures of our own time an easier problem. The present-day painter, it is true, knows something more about the stability of his pigments than did the Impressionists. If he cannot pretend that his paints made with these pigments are better or more honest than theirs, at least he can boast that he knows which of the pigments are permanent.

Even with this, the painter has still not the slightest idea how to paint a picture he can be certain will last more than fifty years. For the stability of pigments is but a small part of a picture's lasting. If a color fades, there still remains a faded picture, but if what holds the colors together should decay, then there is nothing left but some string and splinters and a pinch of tinted dust. How well the picture lasts depends more on what the dust is painted on, and what it has been mixed with to hold it there, than whether the dust itself is constant. Of all these things, oil, canvas, varnish, glue, and how they must be used if the image they hold fixed is to have a reasonable span of life, the painter has little certain knowledge. Not since the break-up of the guilds has there been any properly collated body of practical information about the technique of painting. Formerly one of the functions of the painters' guilds was to record how pictures were made. If a trick worked, it was remembered; if it did not work, it was remembered that it was not to be used. The guilds, besides, were interested in solid craftsmanship and had regulations to control the purity of the painter's materials.

But today, as far as I know, there is no check which operates in the painter's interest on the manufacturers of artist's materials. The painter has no way to assure himself of the quality of the paint and canvas he is sold. Even if he makes his own painting materials, as many painters do, he still must buy his oils and pigments, his turpentine, glue and resins and he cannot be sure of their quality either. He has no longer the inheritance of a body of traditional and tested formulas he can depend on for making his paints and priming his canvas. He is more than likely to experiment with all sorts of strange materials and mixtures, for no better reason than that he has seen them mentioned in some book or other, and this without systematic check on his experiments or record of his results. The book he most depends on, in this country at any rate, is Max Doerner's *Materials of the Artist*. This pretends to be a complete compendium of all the techniques of Western painting, although, in fact, little is known about the methods of the old masters which is either exact or usable. Whatever the book may be in its original German, its English translation is vague, appears to give contrary advice in consecutive sentences, and furnishes authority for almost any mixture or practice.

It is guides such as these, and Doerner is not the most unreliable, that the painters of today must follow in their experiments in immortality. They are urged to paint with egg, temperas and emulsions; with mixtures of egg, oil, varnish, wax, soap, paste, milk and glue; with new pigments like thalo green and titanium white; with air brushes, glazing techniques, soft and hard resin paints, Maroger's medium and black oil; with synthetic varnishes and aluminum painting grounds; with water glass, albertol, phenol-formaldehyde and silicon-tetrachloride and even with luminous paint. When we remember the welter of unsystematic experimentation the painters of the mid-nineteenth century were tempted to indulge in, we cannot be surprised if the painters of the mid-twentieth should be playing with materials that are equally untested.

The permanence of a picture depends on the painter being able to know in advance what will happen twenty years from now to the processes and materials he is using. This in turn depends on keeping records of methods and maintaining standards of materials. Nothing like this exists today. New technical discoveries are made in the laboratories of the big paint and dye companies, leak over into painting, and are adopted by the artist with an easy grace and a complete lack of information about their suitability. New fashions in technique come in, and one fashion follows another with the same seeming irresponsibility as the changes in women's dress. In the early 20's there was an almost universal fashion among the Modern painters for sand. They mixed sand, and even small gravel, in their paint to give texture to their pictures. This fashion went out of style and it was followed by a fashion in wax. Pictures were painted with wax dissolved in the painting medium, or with wax emulsions, or with melted beeswax mixed with the colors as they came out of the tube, the palette all the while kept warm over an electric stove. Christian Bérard executed his most astonishing group of portraits in a heavy, smooth impasto obtained with melted beeswax candles. By certain other painters, the final varnishing of pictures was abandoned, and pictures instead were rubbed with a paste of wax and turpentine and then polished. All this has now gone out of style, and twenty years later, with no records kept, it is impossible to know whether it was good or bad. Not long ago all pictures were varnished with copal varnish—a tough resin dissolved in oil—on the grounds that copal is the hardest of the varnishes and would best protect the picture. Later copal was discarded in favor of mastic resin dissolved in spirits of turpentine on the grounds that mastic varnish is soft and can be easily removed when it goes bad. Then dammar came into fashion, on the grounds that, unlike mastic, it does not develop opaque blue spots of "bloom" (I suspect, however, that it yellows more rapidly). Now the synthetic resin varnishes have come in.

"Synthetic" is the magic word of modern times, bringing to mind all the romance of the laboratory and all the promise of the world of tomorrow. A resin so named is deemed perfect; it cannot yellow or decay like resins found in nature. But this is not necessarily true. Even if the synthetic resins prove perfect in this respect, they have another serious disadvantage. They are extremely tough. To get them into solution, strong solvents like acetone must be used. These solvents are capable of dissolving a modern paint film. So that when these synthetic resin varnishes are to be applied, they must be sprayed on the surface of the picture with an atomizer, and that with the utmost care. Otherwise the varnish will dissolve the painted surface. When such varnishes deteriorate, as I have no doubt eventually they will, they will probably be quite impossible to remove. The restorers, however, must have good reasons for trusting them, for one of these synthetics was used by the Metropolitan, after a recent cleaning of Rembrandt's portrait of his wife, *Saskia as Bellona*. How such a varnish is to be removed if it goes bad, I do not know, unless, as is likely, both Rembrandt's paint film and his public reputation are by now firm enough to withstand any solvent whatsoever.

The trouble with all these experiments is not that any one is necessarily bad. The trouble is that none of the results is ever recorded. There is no continuity of practical knowledge. Methods change too fast. Materials are not the same. A picture goes bad and everybody has forgotten why. The restorers themselves whom one imagines in this too fluid field as having some stable knowledge and able to help the painter ward off changes in his painting, are perhaps as tempted to experiment and as subject to fashion as everybody else.

It is the changes in Whistler's pictures which particularly arouse my curiosity. The pigments he is supposed to have used sound safe enough. Whistler was obviously the possessor of an acute sense of the amenities of color. The titles to all his pictures boast of it. These *Harmonies* and *Symphonies* could only have been in the most refined colors in their most carefully adjusted combinations. Even the title to his celebrated portrait of his mother is properly *An Arrangement in Gray and Black*. Most of these pictures have by now lost their freshness. *The Pacific* in the Frick Collection has no longer the charm of color which must have been the reason for its so slight existence. The *Cremona Gardens* is now invisible. The rose and gray of *Mrs. Leland* are the saddest of relics, like a flower in the yellowed leaves of a forgotten book, melancholy and disquieting. Standing before these pictures I begin to believe with Manet that, after all, black is the most beautiful of all the colors. Black, at any rate, should be safe.

CHAPTER NINE

THE PAINTER AND HIS SUBJECT

A good painter is to paint two main things, namely man and the workings of man's mind.

The Note Books of Leonardo da Vinci

In austere academic circles today it is not fashionable to talk about the subject matter of a picture. The most damning thing that can be said about a picture is to call it "an illustration." Nevertheless, no one, no one at all, will bother about a picture of something he is not interested in, no matter how well it may be painted. The painter may be interested only in the technique of his picture, but the buyer is interested only in what the picture expresses. Consequently, the subject matter of painting always reflects with the utmost exactitude the spiritual and intellectual preoccupations of the painter's time.

In the Middle Ages, under the influence of Greek and Byzantine theology, the subject matter of painting had been the majesty of God, of Christ enthroned as judge, the glory of the saints and the immutability of moral law—a complete and grandiose and terrifying cosmography. In the thirteenth century the Western world began to open up. Italians and other Europeans found they could use the post and caravan routes of the Mongol Empire all the way to the Far East. Marco Polo, a contemporary of Giotto, visited regions of Central Asia which were not revisited by Europeans until the mid-nineteenth century. Palestine, once a remote and romantic goal, was now a part of the workaday business world of Venetian and Genoese merchants. It became apparent to everyone that the Holy Land was a place like any other, with mountains, roads and people—perhaps like Italy, even. A new burgher class, enriched by trade, was replacing the provincial aristocrats who had looked to conservative Byzantium for their taste in art. Abstract theology and the rigid formulisms of Byzantine iconography began to disappear from painting, and its subject matter became, with Giotto and his followers, the humanization of the life of Christ.

Later there came into the West the great body of Greek literature, a new and marvelous testament, teaching new prides, new pleasures, and a new sense of the importance of the individual. And with the Renaissance the painters found what was perhaps their grandest subject—man, his variety, dignity and stature. Later the subject was extended. The Reformation added the Common Man; the Counter-Reformation, The Saintly Man; the eighteenth century, The Reasonable Man and The Man of Sentiment; and, at the end of the century, under the influence of the Romantics, Man as Poet. With the expansion of science in the nineteenth century, the painter's subject became the visible world and its depiction according to the laws of science, its new discoveries about light, color and vision. On these interests Impressionism flourished.

At the end of the nineteenth century, the painter was again in need of a subject. All the old subjects had worn thin. The Greek and Latin classics, so inspiring in Renaissance times, had lost their salt and shock. Man and his grandeurs were no longer convincing. The eighteenth century's Reasonable Man seemed now only modish and affected; the Romantic Man merely silly. The world as it appeared to the Romantic had been vulgarized and corrupted by two generations of official academic painters. Nature as seen by the disinterested eye of science had lost its novelty and most of its interest. Science, for the painter, was at once too trite and too frightening a subject, already threating to become the terrifying antagonist we now find it today. It had already robbed man of his natural and rightful size. Man was no longer the center of the universe, although he was not yet threatened with being pushed entirely off the stage. Repelled by a universe of chilly certainty, the painters, at the beginning of the twentieth century, sought a subject in another and more human of man's works, in art itself. The subject matter of painting in the twentieth century became the picture and its composition.

Here, as always, the painters were reflecting the philosophic preoccupations of their time. In the vast, sprawling, amorphous world the twentieth century introduced, one of the most pressing questions facing philosophers was the problem of the organism. The science and philosophy of the nineteenth century had removed purpose from the universe. Things do, nevertheless, act together as if there were a purpose. Organization, in the universe and in the animal, does seem to exist. A group of individual cells, or men, or stars, does operate together as if it was an organized unit. What constituted this unity was the problem of the philosophers. This is the problem of style, of structure, of the individual, independent, indivisible body—the problem of the organic whole.

The composition of the picture—or rather of pictures in general—offers the painter precisely the same problem. The picture he is making is a unit. It is this unity which wins for the picture a life of its own independent of its maker. And how such a unity is obtained became the fecundating problem of all that twentieth century painting now known (by the name under which it first appeared) as Modern Art. Its great discovery was the application to the making of pictures of one of the most powerful instruments of mathematical analysis developed in the nineteenth century—the method of the alternative hypothesis, of the hypothesis which goes against common sense.

This method, I believe, first appeared as a criticism of Euclid. Euclid stated as a theorem in his geometry that one line, and one line only, can be drawn through a point parallel to another line. This theorem no one had been able to prove so it had been accepted as an axiom. Several of the nineteenth century mathematicians then conceived the idea of supposing the axiom to be false. By assuming the apparently nonsensical idea that no line at all can be drawn through a point parallel to another line, or the equally absurd one that any number of such parallels are possible, these mathematicians were able to construct two logical and self-consistent geometries from which our modern field physics have been derived. By supposing that "a" times "b" is not necessarily equal to "b" times "a," mathematicians have derived various algebras, quite unlike the algebras we learned in school, and along with them some extremely important methods of analysis. The whole of Einstein comes, in fact, from abandoning the perfectly natural assumption that a line at rest has necessarily the same length it has when it is in motion.

Modern Art was arrived at by exactly the same method—by questioning one of painting's basic assumptions, an assumption which had heretofore always appeared self-evident. By abandoning the idea that a picture is necessarily a picture of something, the Modern painters were able to take the composition of pictures as their subject matter, and with this subject produce the most interesting and the most valuable painting done in the first two decades of the twentieth century.

Composition is of prime importance to any painter, Modern or otherwise. The picture, if it is to have a life of its own, must begin by being an indivisible unit. Each part of it is equally important. All its parts must be executed at the same time. A painting cannot be done detail by detail. It must grow all at once, as an organic whole, so that if at any time the painter's work is interrupted, the picture will nevertheless be complete, each part in place, all equally finished, equally expressive and equally interdependent. As Whistler said, a masterpiece is finished from the beginning. Changes made when a picture is too far advanced, when its structure is already set, no matter how skillfully done, will inevitably be as visible, as brutal and as artificial as the changes made by plastic surgery on the features of a face.

This organic, interdependent growth of a picture, these interlocking and mutually dependent lines, shapes and colors, this subordination of the parts to the whole, is composition. Composition is not, perhaps, the picture's essential life. That depends on the vitality of the man who painted it and on the vigor of his ideas. But since it is composition which gives emphasis, shape and clarity to the painter's expression of his ideas, it is largely the picture's composition which renders it capable of being remembered. The spectator, of course, need not be aware that the picture is composed at all. But unless the composition is right, any picture, no matter how skillfully painted, soon gets tiresome to look at. A good picture, by any system of aesthetics or values one can possibly employ, is only a picture that can be looked at with pleasure, and remembered with pleasure, again and again. And this is precisely a consequence of the simplicity and directness with which the painter's ideas are presented—in other words, of the picture's composition.

The Impressionists had not been particularly interested in composition. Let us say rather that they were not particularly interested in its formal elaboration, especially since rules for composition made up a large part of the official academic painting tradition against which they were in revolt. The Impressionist doctrine of equalized surface tension with its unified surface gave their pictures a sufficient organic unity. And the camera, whose way of seeing provided the model for their painting, does not, of itself, compose. It takes nature unprepared. When the Impressionists found that they needed a more formal sort of composition than such casual means provide, the Japanese system of occult balance, with the addition of a convention of perspective, was quite enough. This system of composition known as "occult balance"—offsetting the small crowded areas of a picture by large empty ones—works perfectly well as long as the entire surface of the picture has the same character—the dry paint surface of a Vuillard, for example, or the ink-stamped paper of a Japanese print. And if the empty spaces still appear too empty, they can always be explained and filled by a few perspective lines indicating the boards of a floor, the edges of a cornice or the gutters of a street. So that the casual *mise-en-page* of a camera's view finder, the surface unity provided by an equalized paint texture, occult balance, and a convention of perspective, were all the compositional devices the Impressionists needed—Pissarro, Sisley, Monet, Toulouse-Lautrec, Van Gogh, Vuillard, Bonnard, and the rest. Degas made especially brilliant use of these devices, along with everything else that came his way—Degas, who as I have said before, was not an Impressionist at all, although he made use of all the Impressionist techniques, but was in reality the greatest academician since Ingres and the direct descendant of Poussin.

But Cézanne found these devices for composition not enough. Cézanne knew that the human eye is not the innocent eye of the camera; the world of nature has more dimensions than the simple camera's vision can record. He wished to make of Impressionism, as he said, something comparable to the art of the museums—to Poussin, Rubens, Veronese and the like. For this, the simple act of composition which consists in placing the objects to be painted within a rectangular frame, the camera's view of nature, will not suffice. He needed a more dramatic, a more intense sort of pictorial organization. This he achieved by the use of a set of astounding and original inventions. He conventionalized his color and his drawing, as well as his brush stroke. He limited the space, the depth, the distance back and forth, within his picture. He systematically increased the size of distant objects and diminished the near-by ones to fit more nearly the world our motor senses perceive, which know that a distant and a near-by man have both an equal stature. Most important of all, he abandoned the usual classical perspective which depends on the convention of one fixed, unmoving eye, for a more naturalistic one—for the perspective a painter actually observes with his two eyes and with the slightly shifting point of view he takes before his model.

The compositions that Cézanne arrived at by the use of these devices are still so powerful today that we are prone to forget his skill as a draughtsman and his charm as a colorist. We remember him chiefly on account of the variety and power of his pictorial organizations. These, when they were new, seemed even more astonishing. The young painters at the beginning of the century found them enormously impressive, and through them became interested in the problems of pure composition.

Thus Cézanne can almost be said to be the father of Modern Art. As early as 1909 Braque and Picasso had begun to imitate, explore and further conventionalize Cézanne's conventions of drawing and perspective. As examples there are Picasso's bowl of fruit and Braque's little landscape of a road near L'Estaque, both at the Museum of Modern Art of New York. These painters were already interested in stylistic analysis, as can be seen from their pictures of 1906 and '07 that imitate the mannerisms of Negro sculpture. But these African pictures have little of the real style, unity and beauty the later Cubist pictures possess. And Cubism itself came out of Cézanne. It was also through Cézanne that Duchamp, Juan Gris, Gleizes and all the others became interested in solving the problems of composition by methods of analysis and abstraction.

"Composition," however, is perhaps too simple a word for what these painters were doing. To speak more exactly, their subject matter was art itself—how pictures are built. Their aim was to isolate the essential qualities of character and of structure in a picture which makes it a work of art. What is it, independent of the idea a picture communicates, regardless of the story it tells, purely through the balance of its lines and masses, through its shapes abstracted from any meaning; what makes the picture interesting to look at and makes us continue to find it interesting? What is it that makes a simple dolphin inscribed on a bronze discus as moving to us and as memorable as the most beautiful face? This, essentially, is the problem of composition.

Even poets took composition as their subject matter. The principal poets in English who explored this field were James Joyce and Gertrude Stein. Joyce is scarcely a pure example. In spite of his well-known imitation of the shapes and structure of the Odyssey and the Old Testament in his *Ulysses* and *Finnegans Wake*, his subject matter is not just composition, but rather his education. His obscurities are chiefly literary references unfamiliar to the reader. But if the books Joyce read are known, and the many languages he knew (some learned while teaching in a Berlitz school in Trieste) are understood, all the obscurities become plain.

As Picasso is said to have remarked when he refused to illustrate *Ulysses*, "He is an obscure writer all the world can understand."

But in the case of Gertrude Stein, since the subject matter of her poems is composition itself, its communication is essentially obscure, and cannot by any labor of scholarship even partly be explained. There are, of course, many puns and personal references, some of which can be deciphered. For example, a poem entitled "Suzy Asado," after a Spanish dancer whom she knew, whose name rhymes with "*leche helada*," so that in another poem she becomes (since *asado* in Spanish means "roasted"): "Toasted Suzy is my ice cream." But even if all such references could be tracked down and understood, they would explain very little. Because Gertrude Stein's subject matter —at any rate in the poems which form the greater part of her work—is purely composition in sound. There is, for example, a "Portrait of F.B." which has the same cadences and the same shape as the final poem "Rooms" of *Tender Buttons*. But the actual words used in the two poems are completely different. This is exactly the sort of thing a painter of the time might have done—different versions of the same composition constructed with different still-life objects or with different colors.

Most certainly the early Cubist still-lifes of Picasso and Braque cannot be regarded very seriously as real attempts to depict in multiple perspective their half-legible objects—the folded newspaper, the bottle, the goblet, the guitar, the pipe and the package of Virginia tobacco on a table top. They are rather the use of these conventional

ꞌENUS AND MARS

l Veronese

ılanned picture." Its de- and chiaroscuro were ɔleted in monochrome ꞌe the surface colors were d.

Courtesy of M. Knoedler Gallery

PORTRAIT
ƆF A YOUNG MAN

Bronzino

ine example of precise acterization. Every detail ɔstume and accessory aids efining the subject's per- lity, tastes and social po- n.

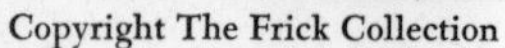

Copyright The Frick Collection

SELF-PORTRAIT

by Rembrandt van Rijn

An intimate portrait. The largement of the left h forces the spectator to st at a distance of easy conve tion with the subject, si only from such a posit does the distortion look ural.

Copyright The Frick Collection

MISS MARY EDWARD

by William Hogarth

An English woman by first English portrait mast Like his literary contem rary Defoe, Hogarth used models objectively.

GENERAL JOHN BURGOYNE

Sir Joshua Reynolds

portrait more in the Noble
ıan in the Grand Style. The
ft hand and waistcoat, un-
nished, show the gray "dead"
ainting.

Copyright The Frick Collection

Courtesy of the Yale University Art Gallery

ELIZABETH STORER SMITH

John Singleton Copley

n American wine-mer-
ıant's wife, hence the grapes.
'he acute characterization
ıd the scrupulous detail mark
ıe provincial painter.

Courtesy of Mrs. Harrison Williams Collection

PORTRAIT OF PEPITO COSTA Y BONELLO

by Francesco Goya

This is Grand Style from t cultural provinces, uninfl enced by French conventio of charm. Painted in Fran or England, the little b would have shown a smile.

ODALISQUE

by Domenique Ingres

An unfinished work con pleted only in gray unde painting. It looks very muc like its photograph.

Courtesy of the Metropolitan Museum of New

THE COUNTESS OF CLANBRASSIL

Sir Anthony Van Dyke

an Dyke's courtly style, re-
ıed from Rubens, for inter-
tional high-life portraiture.
ne would scarcely think this
ly English.

Copyright The Frick Collection

Copyright The Frick Collection

MOTHER AND CHILD

Auguste Renoir

:ench bourgeois comfort
ıd pride. All edges are soft,
:cept for the accented eyes,
e "windows of the soul."
he color, I think, has not
ood up.

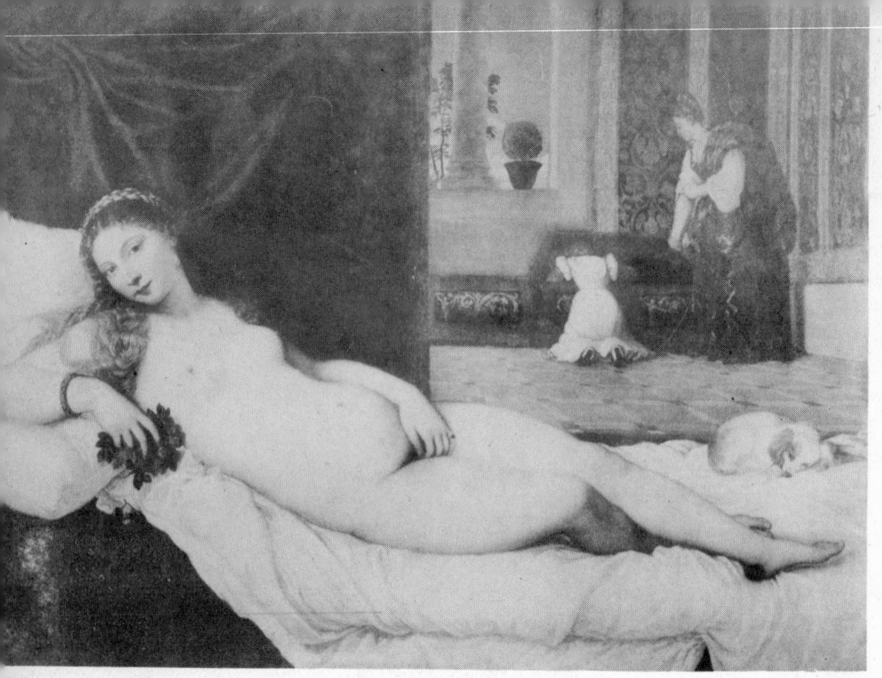

Courtesy of the Uffizi Gallery

THE VENUS OF URBINO **by Titian**

Venus with the head of Eleanora de Gonzaga. The drawing is "sculptural," not "photographic."

OLYMPIA **by Edouard Manet**

A nineteenth-century parody of the above, but a parody of the subject only. "Photographic," not "sculptural" drawing. A perfectly balanced composition, a masterpiece of the brush-stroke school.

Courtesy of the Louvre Gallery

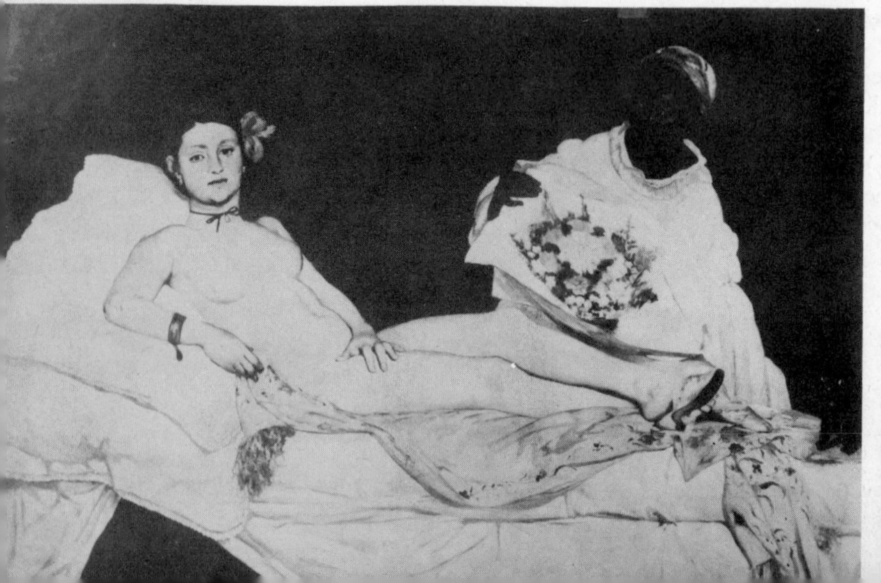

THE DUCHESS OF MARLBOROUGH AND HER SON

by Giovanni Boldini

Apotheosis of the virtuoso brush stroke by the most elegant of Edwardian painters.

Courtesy of the Metropolitan Museum of New York

NUDES BATHING

by A. W. Bouguereau

A popular subject by the most popular nineteenth-century master of the invisible brush stroke and leader of French Academic Painting.

Photograph by courtesy of James Graham and Sons

Courtesy of The National Gallery of Art, Washington, D. C.
(Chester Dale Collection—Loan)

MADAME RENEE DEG

by Edgar Degas

Executed in pale tones of
and gray. From the small
of the figure, one knows
the subject has been vie
from a distance of at least
feet.

Courtesy of the Museum of Modern Art of New York

PINES AND ROCKS

by Paul Cézanne

Such tightness of composit
is characteristic of this mas
The triangles and vertic
prefigure Cubism.

NUDE DESCENDING A STAIRCASE (Version of 1917)

Marcel Duchamp

nlike the work of the classi-
l Cubists, this picture is not
atic. Multiple image is used
 represent motion. In Italy,
 similar development was
lled Futurism.

urtesy of The Louise and
alter C. Arensberg Collection
e Philadelphia Museum of Art

"MA JOLIE" (Woman with Guitar)

y Pablo Picasso

lassical Cubism derived from
ézanne's tightly packed com-
osition, architectural, static
nd self-contained.

Courtesy of the Museum of Modern Art
of New York

Courtesy of the Museum of Modern Art of New York

FRUIT DISH

by Pablo Picasso

A conventualization of the Cézanne still-life. Instead of representing particular objects, Picasso evokes the elements of a famous still-life style.

Courtesy of the Museum of Modern Art of New York

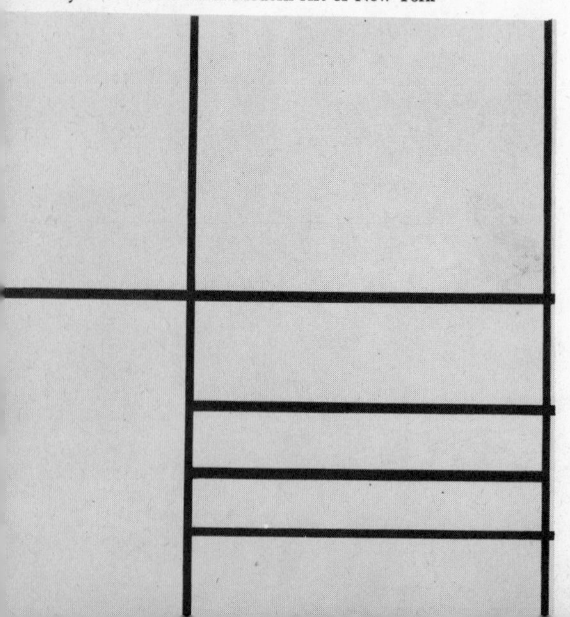

COMPOSITION IN WHITE, BLACK AND RED

by Piet Mondrian

The end-product of the analysis of composition. Of particular interest to architects and industrial designers.

Courtesy of the Museum of Modern Art of New York

COMPOSITION VII, FRAGMENT I by Wassily Kandinsky

Emotional composition in paint, done on the discipline of spontaneity. Kandinsky strongly influences today's abstract painters.

BOAT LANDING by Paul Klee

This pretends to be a child's painting, but is the work of an extremely sophisticated mind. The artist's subtlety of color and great variety of stylistic resources are not childlike at all.

Photograph by courtesy of the Buchholz Gallery

Courtesy of the Hugo Gallery, Collection of Alexandre Jolas

LA VOIX DU SANG

by René Magritte

A dark blue picture. Insid the tree trunk, a house wit lighted windows. Magritte one of the few Surrealis whose symbolism remains her metic.

Courtesy of the Pierre Matisse Gallery

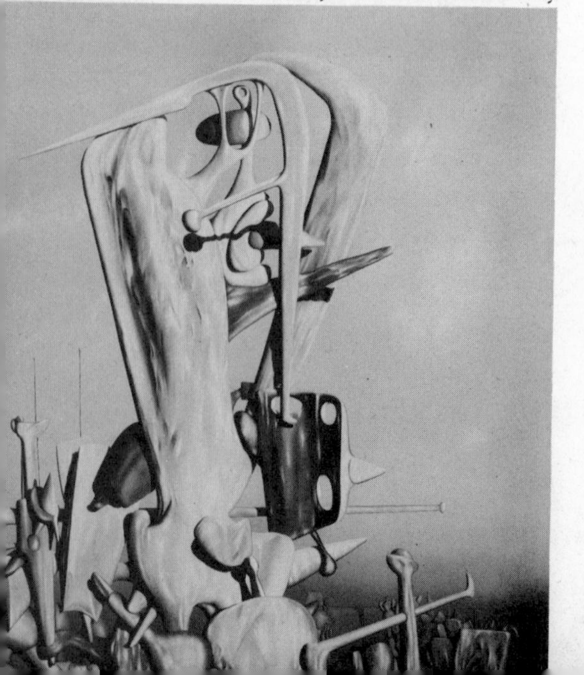

MA VIE BLANCHE ET NOIRE

by Yves Tanguy

Machines inside the mind. Again the discipline of spontaneity.

FLORENTINE SAND-DIGGERS

Leonid

he double image through ıemory. The artist does not ıint exactly what he observes n the spot, but rather what e retains of it in poetic retro- ɔect.

Courtesy of Miss Louise Crane

Courtesy of the Artist

FATA MORGANA

y Pavel Tchelitchew

Vermont mountains which re also a nymph and faun. The multiple image, though a ɔersonal fancy of the painter, s wholly visual, not a verbal- zed concept. The title merely neans "mirage."

YOUNG GIRL WITH FAN

by Christian Bérard

The painter's emotional preoccupations are reflected on the sitter's face, and communicate as powerfully as through a motion-picture close-up.

EGGS

by Maurice Grosser

Eggs that, through enlargement, suggest female forms. Also a close-up.

Courtesy of Boris Kochno

Courtesy of the Museum of Modern Art of New York

THE FOREST

Max Ernst

ɔrdwood surfaced with "rus-:" grainings. Ernst's extraor-nary delight in textures has d him to make pictures out almost every known sub-ance, including paint.

Courtesy of the Museum of Modern Art of New York

Courtesy of the Museum of Modern Art of New York

WINTER

Eugene Berman

he poetry of deserted places. eo - Romanticism contrasts e real outer world with the ainter's own private feelings ɔout it.

Courtesy of the Museum of Modern Art of New York

Courtesy of Mrs. Richard Deutsch

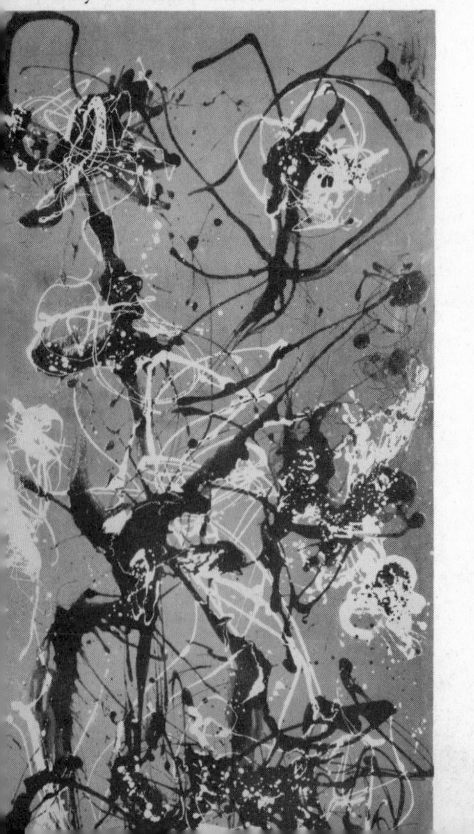

PANCHO VILLA, DEAD AND ALIVE

by Robert Motherwell

The discipline of spontaneity, devised by Kandinsky. The painter's interest is in the elaboration of textures.

NUMBER 10, 1950

by Jackson Pollock

The subject of this picture is the beauty of paint when somewhat accidently laid down. The spontaneity-plus-hazard method applied to a large canvas. There is no image in it, either planned or accidental.

objects for the purpose of making pictures whose subject matter is an analysis of composition. Here the composition is still derived from the pictures of Cézanne, with, however, Cézanne's middle-class and provincial heaviness replaced—in the case of Braque and Picasso at any rate—by a Parisian elegance and lightness of hand. These painters and the others of the Modern school then applied this sort of compositional analysis to other kinds of art, to Roman wall decoration, to Byzantine frescos, to the architectural style of the Manhattan skyscrapers, to early playing cards —to almost any exotic art that came their way. It even became possible to paint completely abstract pictures with apparently no reference whatsoever to the history of painting.

There was nothing new in these painters' painting methods themselves. They still relied on the two technical discoveries of the Impressionists—equalized surface tension and a system of improvising pictures on the spot. The great innovation of these Modern masters was their interest in pure composition. And the essential definition of what is commonly known as Modern painting today, the easiest way Modern Art is to be distinguished from a picture of any other time or school, is simply this: a picture in practically any manner whatsoever whose subject is its own composition.

Like the Impressionists, the Modern painters were influenced by the technical resources of their time. The Impressionists, with their subject matter of how the outside world of nature appears to the innocent eye, had as their chief influence the science of photography. The Modern painters of the early twentieth century, with composition as their subject, had as chief influence the body of art reproductions that had by then become available.

We ourselves forget how short a time such art reproductions have existed. It was not until quite late in the nineteenth century that any photographs of famous paintings began to be made at all. Before this, the only reproductions of pictures to be had were the engravings and oil copies made of them. These, for the most part, were quite inaccurate and reflected more closely the taste of the epoch in which they were made than the actual style of the picture itself. In Victorian copies, Rubens, Guido Reni, and Raphael all look like Mid-Victorian pictures painted by Etty or Winterhalter. But reputable museums willingly bought and hung these copies of the famous paintings, because only through such copies could the paintings be known. Otherwise, to become acquainted with them, one had to endure the labor and expense of travel, and go and stand in front of the pictures. In fact, as late as the 1850's, the whole Pre-Raphaelite movement was well under way before any of its members had seen the paintings they pretended to take as guides, or anything better than some quite inadequate line engravings in a book belonging to Rossetti.

With the turn of the century, however, all this was changed. Photographic reproductions became common. Reproduction became available, not only of European masterpieces, but of all other art as well—of Aztec, Byzantine, Catalonian, Dahomeyan, Etruscan, Finnish, Grecian, Hittite, Indic, Javanese, Kurdish, Ligurian, Moslem, Numidian, Peruvian, Queenslandian, Ruritanian, and so on through the atlas and the alphabet, in brochures, booklets, albums, portfolios, and single prints, all remarkably well made, exhaustive, and inexpensive. Every painter's studio contained them, and he consulted them constantly. Or if he did not have them at home, following a principle of many painters who refuse to have a picture on the wall, even one of their own, so as not to be continually disturbing their visual sensibilities, he was shown them at the houses of all his friends. These reproductions were at their best in black and white. Color reproductions hardly existed and, if they did, were extremely inaccurate. On account of the difficulties of photography and of publication, the prints were never in proper size—always reductions of large pictures or, at the most, depiction of details. Since most of these prints were taken from the arts of cultures alien to our own, the story they were originally made to tell was usually as incomprehensible to the painter who admired them as if they were books written in an unknown language. He knew nothing of the subject matter of this art or of its iconography. He understood nothing of the emotional implications the subject matter was intended to convey. Consequently, from the reproductions of this exotic art, the painter could get a clear idea neither of its color, size nor meaning. All he was able to learn from these prints was the formal composition of the works of art and the stylistic devices their various artists employed.

To the painter, this universal encyclopedia of art was breath-taking. He was enthralled by the revelation of the unlimited variety of powerful and apparently free ways a visual idea can be expressed. Furthermore, he was perfectly aware that the visual ideas this exotic art contained were not those of our own civilization; that their significance was quite inaccessible to him. Yet the effect of the formal composition of this art, alone, and apparently without any help from the visual ideas that it framed, was so extraordinary, that the young painters were easily persuaded that the important element in all art is its form and not its content. Through these reproductions the Modern painters were confirmed in their choice of composition as subject matter for their painting, and aided as well in their pictorial researches.

The subject matter itself was so original and arresting that the Modern painters immediately found their public. Hitherto, the public for painting has always been made up of people of all kinds of intellectual attainments, having in common only that they liked to look at pictures. But the public for the new Modern art had this peculiarity: it was exclusively an intellectual public, interested in intellectual and literary novelty, and organized and led by the advanced poets.

For a poet to be a painter's press agent is nothing new. Pietro Aretino had acted in this capacity for Titian, and it is perhaps for this reason that Titian painted Aretino so many times. But Modern painting had even more poets connected with it than is generally the case, certainly more than had been associated with Impressionism. In the beginning there were Max Jacob, Guillaume Apollinaire and Gertrude Stein. The poets Jean Cocteau, André Breton, Louis Aragon, Paul Eluard and many others directed its later development. These poets were not only press agents for the painting itself. They promoted the careers of the various painters and acted as expert advisers on style, subject matter and iconography. Under such generalship, and with the startling nature of the subject matter itself, Modern Art sprang into immediate prominence. Only a few years after its inception, it had acquired enthusiastic collectors, prosperous dealers, a sky-rocketing market and world-wide fame.

Very few of the amateurs of Modern Art, I imagine, actually understood what the pictures were about. This, however, made little difference to their pleasure. Understanding means very little in connection with painting. One can easily accept a picture, like or dislike it—at any rate, remember it—without really understanding its subject matter. When someone says he understands a Rembrandt and does not understand a Duchamp, he means only that he is used to the sight of the one and not of the other. And for these Modern painters, it was in no way necessary that they be understood. The very novelty, the shock value itself, of the pictures convinced their admirers. The reason is not hard to find. Again the source is in the pictures of Cézanne.

Degas had pointed out Cézanne to Vollard, the picture dealer, as the most important of the Impressionists. Vollard became Cézanne's merchant and his collector as well. Accustomed as we are today to the work of Cézanne, it is difficult for us to understand how shocking this painting seemed in 1890, how ugly, purposeless and incompetent. The critics of the time (they can be found in old copies of *The International Studio*) speak of his bad drawing, his ignorance of the simplest laws of perspective, his heavy color, his lumpy paint surface, his canvases left carelessly unfinished, even in part uncovered, his minor talent as a still-life painter, his monstrous nudes. Vollard tells of a husband punishing his wife, presumably for infidelity, by holding her and forcing her to look at a Cézanne nude, to demonstrate to her how repulsive is the flesh and how ugly was what she had been doing. Cézanne was admitted to be a charming water-colorist. But his oils the critics dismissed: he knew neither how to paint nor how to draw. This was, I suspect, even Vollard's secret opinion as well—not that this would have made any difference to so intelligent and resourceful a picture merchant.

But Degas had been right. By the time of Cézanne's death his picture prices were soaring. Ten years later, he was admitted by all to have been the greatest of the Impressionists—he was even called a Post-Impressionist—and the father of Modern Art. His importance could not be mistaken. His former incomprehensibility, it was realized, had been the natural result of his profound originality. Consequently, it was decided that anything that was incomprehensible was a work of talent, and anything that remained incomprehensible for a very long time was a work of genius—which, after all, is not too bad an idea.

So that it profited the Modern painters enormously by being hard to understand. Braque and Picasso, in particular, kept their public puzzled, interested and convinced by changing the style of their pictures every several years; or rather by changing the school of art whose composition they were analyzing and using as subject. The real and continued success of these painters, however, was not due to any such trick of merchandising. It came from the genuine quality of their painting and from the vitality of their subject matter. Even today this subject matter has not yet lost its importance. The world we live in, the world the twentieth century introduced, is complex to the point of appearing purposeless and disorganized. In such a world, organization and composition are the most reassuring of endeavors, and hand-work the rarest of luxuries. Hand-work and composition was what these Modern painters provided.

So, it is not surprising that Modern Art has maintained its prestige even today. Since its inception, other painting subjects have been tried, and other schools of painting have arisen. But it is only the pictures of the classical Modern painters, of Picasso, Braque, Matisse, Duchamp, and the others, all of them young painters in Paris at the beginning of the century, that today have high and firmly established prices. All of these pictures have three things in common: first, they were done with a most skillful and sensitive hand as free improvisations. Next, their paint surfaces are composed with an eye to balance and equilibrated emphasis in the paint itself. The paint stays flat on the canvas and defines its plane. As Cocteau said, speaking of these Modern pictures, a picture is not a window. A Modern picture was constructed, instead, to be an object, all of whose parts were to be equally interesting. And finally, the picture's real subject is its own composition, although it may have as virtual subject a double image or a visual pun.

These were the three unities of classical Modern Art. Their presence defines a Modern picture, for they were not assembled before 1906, nor strictly observed by any of the painters who began to be known after 1925. The intellectual respectability of these unities is so great that today all our colleges and universities can include painting in the Modern manner as a course of study on a par with philosophy or pure mathematics. And the market value of the

Modern pictures painted under the canon of these unities is so firmly established that many museums have been erected in their honor. Indeed, Modern Art is the only school of painting that has ever been thus signally distinguished. There are a number of these museums of Modern Art—there is even one today in Paris—built to house the Modern pictures which form the principal values of their collections.

These Modern pictures, to be exact, are pictures painted by the school of Paris, generally in Paris itself, between 1903 and 1925. In the Modern museums these particular pictures are, of course, supplemented by the later work of the Modern masters and by the work of our own contemporaries. Actually, however, the Modern museums have little to do with the work not directly influenced by the Modern masters. This is not surprising. After all, a museum is essentially only a collection of objects whose value, with the passage of time, has now become established, and whose importance, consequently, can now be estimated and esteemed. So that a museum, no matter how modern, can operate only with those objects which are our recognized heritage from the past. The precise difference between Modern Art and contemporary art, moreover, has never been accurately defined. And the directors of these Modern museums, by an understandable misapprehension, consider that Modern Art is still as contemporary today as it was in 1918. Any resistance to Modern Art they take to be a middle-class, conservative and ignorant reaction. Consequently they have done little to encourage any but the officially recognized Modern masters, or the painting visibly derived from the canons of Modern Art. These they publicize by means of booklets, reproductions, exhibitions fixed and traveling, and by popular lectures, all centered around the collections of Modern pictures they themselves possess. Thus they are constantly engaged in demonstrating that Modern Art is still the painting of today, and that any contemporary painting not connected with Modern Art is a negligible and reactionary trend.

With such forces, it is not surprising that Modern Art, first championed by the Modern poets, has now become the official academic art of our century, an academy as imperious and as intolerant as the academy of the 70's which rejected the Impressionists. This academy is composed of the Modern museums, the Modern painters and their followers, their dealers and collectors, as well as the great body of instructors who teach painting by the methods of Modern Art. As usual with an academy, it regards any departure from its official canons of non-meaning as severely as the Salon of 1874 judged a picture which neglected to tell a story.

But composition as a subject matter for painting has, for the painter, several serious drawbacks. To begin with perhaps the least, it is not a satisfactory subject matter for large pictures. This, of course, can also be said of the subject matter of the Impressionists, of the camera's view of nature. The early Renoirs, it is true, are large. And the pictures of Bonnard and Vuillard are frequently enormous. Degas and Seurat I do not count. Although they used the Impressionist techniques, both painted planned pictures. But the pictures, at any rate, the best pictures, of Cézanne, Pissarro, Sisley, Van Gogh, Mary Cassatt, Monet and the others are all with few exceptions small enough to have been carried under the painter's arm to the spot where they were painted. Monet's one ambitious project, his murals of water lilies in the Hôtel de Ville at Rouen, is in no way a success.

But composition is even less satisfactory a subject matter for large pictures than the subject of the Impressionists. A private conversation between the painter and his muse, it is even more restricting than the exact observation of nature, and can only with difficulty be broadcast to a large and public audience. It is too personal for this. It gives even less excuse than scientific exactitude or water lilies for large, heroic paintings. The Modern painters, like all painters who wish to make their canvases visible in large public exhibitions, were obliged to paint large pictures. But for the most part, the large Modern pictures are not large pictures in the way that Veronese's pictures, or Gozzoli's, are large. *The Marriage at Cana*, for instance, could not be reduced even slightly without losing much of its effect. But most of the large Modern pictures are only small pictures blown up to exposition size. The compositions of Gleizes gain nothing by their enlargement. Ozenfant's ten-foot jugs would be less oppressive perhaps as post cards. The pictures of Picasso are usually much larger than one would imagine from the photographs. His pictures inspired by the ballets of 1925, these tender couples with their classically straight noses, look in the photographs like pleasant eight by tens. They are indeed eight by tens but measured in feet rather than in inches. Few of the Picassos painted after the second decade of the century are large pictures in the sense that his earlier *Saltimbanques* in Chicago is a large picture, where the size of the picture and the size of the canvas exactly coincide, and the largeness of the canvas was necessary to give the painter all his ease. On the contrary the large pictures Picasso painted after the First World War are for the most part only small pictures spread thin, with little pictorial excuse for their expansion. They seem in their extended emptiness intended as posters advertising Modern Art rather than as pictures to be lived with. In fact, most of the more ambitious pictures of all the Modern masters, admirably adapted as they are for public exhibition, can only with the greatest difficulty be introduced into a private home. Imagine the *Guernica* in your living room, or Matisse's *Dance* in the front hall.

The greatest drawback, however, to composition as a subject matter for painting is that it limits the painter's public and his market to the intellectual or, so to speak, the literary world.

As I have said before, it is the subject matter of a picture that the public is first interested in. That is what the public, at any rate the public of the painter's own time, is buying. How the subject is presented—how a picture is to be built around it—is a preoccupation of the painter alone. A layman, of course, cannot be associated with pictures for any length of time without acquiring some knowledge about the ways that pictures are painted, and a feeling about the various painters' relative skills. Nevertheless, it is no more necessary for a picture lover to know how a picture was produced than for a motorist to know what goes on under the hood of his automobile. What is required of both the picture and the automobile is that they work—that the automobile go fast and safely and that the picture tell its story with conviction and illustrate the preoccupations of its age.

But the story it tells must not be a trivial one. It must be the most noble and the most engrossing concept of the painter's time. The laws of God, Christ as man, man as demi-god, mankind in its varieties, nature seen through the eyes of a poet, the description of the visible world according to the laws of science—all these are subjects that have had enormous interest for the painter's various publics. But analytical composition, in the long run, is of interest only to the painter himself. It is chiefly for this reason, almost for this reason alone, that the market for the painter's pictures has become as limited as it is today. It is because of the subject matter these Modern painters chose to illustrate that the painter, by instinct gregarious, has now been driven into the disagreeable position of solitary workman, and into the position, untenable for one who is by taste and training a skilled artisan, of being high priest of aesthetics and sometimes star of publicity.

CHAPTER TEN

PAINTING AS A LIBERAL EDUCATION

Your manner of living should always be regulated as if you were studying theology, philosophy, or any other science; that is to say, eating and drinking temperately at least twice a day, using light but good food, and but little wine; sparing and reserving your hand, saving it from fatigue as throwing stones or iron bars, and many other things which are injurious to the hand, wearying it. There is still another cause, the occurrence of which may render your hand so unsteady that it will tremble and flutter more than leaves shaken by the wind, and this is frequenting too much the company of ladies—— Let us return to our subject.

Advice to painting students, from *The Book of Art of Cennino Cennini*

The medieval universities taught the arts. These were Music, Rhetoric and the various branches of Literature and Poetry. Painting, Architecture and Sculpture they did not teach. These were classed as crafts, not as arts, and it was not until the Renaissance and even later that they acquired this dignity. Even then, they were looked upon as skills to be learned by doing. They did not share the dignity of the Word, and no place was allowed for them in the universities.

Since the Renaissance, the respect accorded these arts has been steadily growing. The universities have long wished to take them over. Music they already have—at least its more intellectually respectable aspects which are the history of music and the technique of composition. They teach that branch of literature known as Creative Writing. Architecture they own as well. Architecture's poor relation, Sculpture, no one seriously needs any longer. The universities teach the history of art and train museum curators. It is in the universities that picture restorers generally receive the first intimation of their vocation. To this list of subjects concerned with the creative arts they have also wished to add the teaching of the practice of painting. But painting, in the form in which it has hitherto been taught, they have not till now been able to absorb. Painting has always been taught better in the specialized art schools. Today, however, the universities have found that painting, if taught in the form of Modern Art, will fit into their usual course of studies.

Not that the universities are capable of teaching painting well. The only subjects they are properly equipped to teach are subjects which can be learned from books. The techniques of the creative arts, which must be learned by doing, under the guidance of someone who has himself learned how they are done, are among the things the universities have always taught very inefficiently, and which today they are perhaps less fitted to teach than heretofore. Even in their own subjects, they have been forced, by the tripling and quadrupling of enrollment during the last thirty years, to a sort of mass production of learning. They have been obliged, much against their will, to suppose that what one man can teach to four or five students, he can teach equally well to four or five hundred. They have had to streamline their courses of instruction for interchangeable professors and for examinations whose questions can be answered by a simple yes or no, and, if necessary, can be graded by a tabulating machine. Under such conditions it is now becoming increasingly difficult for a student in a university to learn to use a foreign language. A student in Philosophy, History, Economics or the Arts finds that he can pass his courses with only a text book, a slight acquaintance with the catalogue of a library and the indices of the books he has been advised to read, and can graduate knowing little about his subject save how to go through the motions of teaching it—and this at a constantly lowering level.

But instruction in an art cannot be thus abbreviated. An art must be learned, not as if it were to be taught to someone else, but as if the art itself were going to be practiced.

Painting, as we all know, was originally taught as a craft in a shop. The students were apprentices. They were taken young, even as young as nine or ten. They were generally boarded at the establishment, shown how to grind colors, to prepare panels and canvas, to lay gold leaf, to draw and to paint, and all this as quickly as possible so that they would be as quickly as possible of some use to their master. By the time they were grown they were able to paint their masterpiece (as their graduation exercise was called), enter into the guild and become masters themselves.

With the prestige painting acquired during the Renaissance this system of apprenticeship changed. Painting began to be regarded as one of the liberal arts and was taught as such, though not yet in the universities. Academies of painting began at Bologna about 1585, and after that painting was something students paid for the privilege of learning. The courses of instruction consisted of some general literary culture, copying well-known pictures and drawing from the antique and the nude. The system of instruction has changed very little from that time to this. This is still the way painting is presented in the professional arts schools today, although drawing from plaster casts and copying old masters has been somewhat frowned on in the last several decades. It is thought to stifle the student's originality.

Painting students, however, only rarely have originality, even the best of them. What they and their teachers are apt to call originality is, in fact, only their facility, the student's ability to make use of tricks and devices he has been able to pick up from the paintings to which he has been exposed. Genuine originality in painting the young rarely possess, the very young never. In this respect, originality in the visual arts is very different from originality in music. Musical talent, and even musical originality, can manifest itself at a very early age. Musical prodigies of four or five are not uncommon. Very frequently they continue to be musical prodigies all the rest of their lives with little change in the character of their talent. There is no radical break, for example, between the music that Mozart wrote as a child and as a man. There is no exact point at which it ceases to be the work of a well-trained, talented and imitative child, and begins to take on the personal expression and original invention the mature Mozart displayed. There is no point at which one can say: here the facility of the child begins to show the character of the man. The one grows out of the other imperceptibly. But painting is different. The painting of a child has nothing at all to do with the painting he may do when he is grown. There is an essential readaptation to space, a necessary reorientation of the ego to the world, which takes place in adolescence and which makes whatever painting the painter may have done as a child of quite a different order, character and intention from his work as a man.

To a child, feeling the outside world is more important than seeing it; his feeling comes before his seeing. The world he draws is the world of motor responses, very like the world of the blind. Everything he draws he puts down in tactile symbols as if he were touching it or counting it with his finger tips. The child does not draw an object as it appears to his eye; he draws instead his muscular memory of the object's shape, number, protuberances and motion. The child draws a head with circles for eyes because the eyeballs are spheres, with a shock of pencil lines for hair, because the hair feels like thin lines or wires. His nose is a triangle with perhaps two holes below—that is the way it seems to the fingers. His mouth has teeth and the ears stick out. He draws a hand with five loops because he can count five fingers. And to make a foot he ends the leg with little lumps for toes. The most important thing about clothes are the buttons, because they are hard, and because they are the way in and out of the clothes he wears. The most important thing about a hat is the brim he can hold on to, and of a train or a wagon, the wheels that go round. Houses have chimneys for smoke, and doors and windows for him to stick his fingers in. And if his house has a fence, it makes little difference to him if in his drawing it may seem to us to lie flat—its function is to go around the house and keep the people in or out. His trees may or may not have leaves —leaves are often too far above his head for him to reach —but it always has a trunk, and sometimes apples and birds. What he draws is not the world he sees, but the world he knows is there.

The drawing of an adult, on the other hand, is visual. It records the outside world as his eye sees it. It classifies the objects according to size, distance, color and apparent shape, and relates them one to another by the conventions of perspective current in his time. The grownup draws, not so much what he knows is there, but what he has learned to see. He draws a world of which he is not the center. It is a world to which he himself belongs as only one of the innumerable elements. This is not the world the child knows. The child cannot—as long as he remains a child—learn to draw like a man. Whatever drawing a child may be able to do in the grown-up style cannot be a picture of the world a grown-up person would see. It will necessarily be an imitation of the mannerisms of grown-up drawing, trite and clever, and of no artistic interest or originality whatsoever.

Nor can a grown-up man draw the world of a child either. The paintings of Paul Klee may take the drawings of children as their subject. But they are neither the drawings that a child would do, nor the work of a man with a childlike mind, nor anything at all like what either would produce. They have too much variety and originality for this. Whereas the drawings of children, however unrestrained their design and color may seem to us to be, possess only the inconsequential originality due to accident. They have for us, of course, the charm of belonging to a world of which we ourselves no longer form a part. But however much our educators and museum people may encourage and admire it, the painting of children is none the less the subject matter of anthropology—not of the history of art.

This child's talent for painting almost all children possess. It invariably disappears at the end of childhood. The grown-up talent for painting, if it is there, begins to manifest itself somewhere in adolescence. The one talent, when it disappears, is frequently replaced by the other. But, there is such a difference in kind between the two sorts of talents that having had a talent for painting in childhood does not seem to advance the post-adolescent painter in any way.

The reason is that the technique of painting depends only on the training of the eye and of the sense of space, and scarcely at all on the sort of training of the memory and the hand which has such an importance in music. The musician must learn his elaborate finger techniques as quickly as possible. The muscular and memory training he receives as a child he will never lose. But muscular agility serves the painter very little. The celebrated story about Giotto's drawing a free-hand circle would prove his talent for painting as little as the story of the cherry tree proves Washington's statesmanship. The painter draws with his eyes, not with his hands. Whatever he sees, if he sees it clear, he can put down. The putting of it down requires, perhaps, much care and labor, but no more muscular agility than it would take for him to write his name. Seeing clear is the important thing. This ability depends on the painter no longer being a child. To see clear, he must have experienced the indispensable wrench of beginning grown-upness which has displaced him from the center of the universe to make him only one of its many terms. The musician's subject matter comes from the tongue he speaks and his own muscular sensations, from the world he feels and listens to inside his own head. In the same way, the writer learns his trade through listening and through speaking. His subject matter may change with age but not his ear. A poet, as they say, is born, not made. But for the painter, seeing clear is an acquired technique. It is not a talent of childhood. It cannot be acquired at all until childhood is past. So, compared to the musician and the poet, the painter gets off to a tardy start. Originality in painting depends on originality of eye and thought. Each eye, each mind, and consequently, each view of the world, is different. Since this is the originality the painter must express, this real, innate originality cannot exist in a student's work until he is sufficiently in command of his brush to be able to express it.

Whether copying pictures is an aid to the expression

of a student's originality or a hindrance to its development is more than I would venture to decide. Nevertheless, the system of painting instruction established by the academies, of copying pictures, drawing from life, and some general education to furnish the mind, has been until recently the only system of art education available. It does not work at all well in the universities.

Not that there is any trouble about literary culture (that is what the universities do best), nor about old masters to copy—there are generally plenty of these in the near-by museums, and universities themselves usually possess collections of their own. But when it comes to introducing the life class among their other courses, the universities run into several practical difficulties.

With the provincial universities there is frequently trouble about the life class itself. The universities understand the importance of the life class in learning to draw; the student who has learned to draw the nude can draw anything. The shape of the human body is the most complicated and subtle thing in the whole world; it is the one thing in the world that everybody knows best. Any fault in its proportions or in its rendering is at once apparent to everybody. But to the provincial colleges, the nude models may sometimes present insuperable social embarrassments. To the popular mind, of which the student body forms a part, the life class hopefully represents an authorized immorality—the reason why, and not the means by which, a painter learns to draw. The universities themselves know that nothing could be more innocent and less romantic than the relation of student and life class model. It is none the less true that provincial universities may well think twice before they present a course of instruction which in the popular mind is the very symbol of temptation and incontinence.

Models, too, are another difficulty. In a small community female models are impossible to obtain. The respectable girls know that once deprived of their clothes in front of their college classmates they have forever lost their glamour. And the girls who are not respectable know that they can gain more money more easily or more steadily elsewhere. There are young men among the student body who can be got to pose. But a male nude in a mixed class is sometimes an even greater affront to provincial respectability than the female.

For the great universities these difficulties do not exist. Here, models can always be found. The public and the students can be taught manners. The life class is set up; then comes the real difficulty—finding someone to teach it. Good drawing teachers are rare and do not fit into the universities.

The subjects ordinarily taught in universities are branches of abstract, generalized knowledge. These demand for their teaching a verbal facility, not a manual skill. Instructors for the normal academic subjects can be adequately trained in the universities themselves. In fact, training of teachers to perpetuate the academic tradition has always been one of the universities' major functions.

But the universities are less happy when it comes to finding instructors for subjects which depend only on complicated skills of hand and eye as do the techniques of the plastic arts—subjects which by their own traditions can be taught only by people who can themselves perform the sleight-of-hand maneuvers and can guide the students by demonstration and example. Here a textbook is of little use, reading assignments serve for nothing, and examinations do not grade the students' progress. In sum, nothing at all in the traditional methods of teaching the applied arts fits either the universities' system of instruction or their system of grades.

So, up till recently, drawing instructors of high professional competence were as out of place in a university as the expert teachers in voice and piano. Most good drawing teachers are painters, and without any college training at all. They will have attended, instead, one of the professional art schools, and seldom have enough academic degrees to run a department in a university, or even to receive a proper salary there. They prefer to teach in the art schools where they can receive the pay and the respect which is their due. The universities themselves have no mechanism for turning out competent drawing instructors from their own ranks. There is not, as far as I know, any textbook or system of study by which an ordinary university graduate can learn to teach drawing without his first having learned to draw. It is this, exactly, which has heretofore limited the painting instruction in the universities—not the difficulties connected with the life classes themselves, but the graver difficulties of finding professors for them. This difficulty has now been obviated. Modern Art has shown the universities a way out—a system of painting instruction requiring no ability in representational drawing, and which can be taught without special talent, ability, or extra-academic training by any properly qualified Ph.D.

This sort of art instruction, as it is given today in the universities, has, from the point of view of the teacher, enormous advantages. No ability either to see or to render the outside world is demanded of student or professor. All that is required is canvas, brushes, colors, an acquaintance with the reproductions of paintings and a knowledge of theoretical aesthetics. Although the differences between Modern Art and contemporary painting have never been formulated, the principles behind Modern Art itself are clearly understood and can be described today as precisely as any other painting or decorative style of the past—as "Art Nouveau," for example. "Art Nouveau," in the early decade of our century, could not be formulated; it was simply the advanced decorative style. But today, now that it is no longer part of our contemporary life, it has become apparent that "Art Nouveau" was a form of Gothic revival characterized by the use of stylized flower forms—iris, tulip, poppy, cattail, water lily and so on, in tertiary colors—dull yellows, mauves, browns and olive greens, and in weak curves—curves which start off to be a spiral and then do something else. The description of Modern Art as a painting style can be made today in terms just as precise. They are, as I have said before: First, the picture must have an equal surface tension so that no one part of it attracts the eye more than another. Second, the picture must be an improvisation. It must seem to have grown spontaneously, as if by inspiration, under the painter's hand, all of its parts advancing equally, each part fluid and capable of being changed and adjusted as the picture progresses, until the composition arrives at its perfect, final state. Third, the composition itself is the subject of the picture.

This composition is either entirely abstract, or has for added interest reference to natural objects. These natural objects, however, are in general not depicted realistically, but must be schematized—perhaps in the style of another school of art—and used as symbols; not as the way the painter sees the outside world, but as building blocks for the construction of the composition. The quality of the finished picture, then, can be judged by the ease of its surface, the elegance of its execution and the perfection of its composition.

All this can be learned in laboratory periods and from textbooks. No top-ranking professional instruction in realistic drawing is required. Thus, with the aid of Modern Art, painting has been able to enter the universities on a par with philosophy, theology or any of the sciences and to be taught with the greatest ease as an intellectual exercise. Since the instructors can now receive most of their training in the universities, they can be accorded academic distinction and can be permitted to run their own departments. Since, in this system of painting instruction, the ability to render objects as they appear to the eye is of little importance, it makes little difference whether drawing is taught badly or well. Drawing instruction being no longer of prime importance, classes in drawing can be offered with whatever means the university has at hand. The courses are relatively easy. Working with paints and color is a delight to anyone. As a result, painting classes in all colleges and universities today are numerous and enthusiastically attended.

The actual painting turned out in these university classes has seldom any serious artistic value. It is, for the most part, not very unlike the stenciled linen, painted china, tooled leather, burned wood, hammered brass and gilded rolling pins which so delighted our immediate ancestors. This, however, is in no way surprising. The few students who are talented enough to think of becoming professional painters acquire their serious professional training elsewhere. The students who major in the field are principally engaged in learning to teach art. Most of the students are enrolled simply because the courses are easy and delightful, although some will later go into commercial art.

No one can have become acquainted with the handling of the painter's materials without becoming interested in the problems of painting and aware of its pleasures and difficulties. No one can paint a picture, no matter how bad, without learning the difference between a real painting and a printed reproduction. Thus, the universities are encouraging an interest in painting that the painter of today cannot afford to disregard. These painting students, this prosperous middle-class student body, which has learned by manipulating paints to look at pictures, most probably will become the painter's next public. Painting today is certainly in need of a new public, now that the last two—the comfortably rich of before the First World War, and the intellectual elite of before the Second—have so completely disappeared.

This system of teaching, with all its advantages, is still more suitable for turning out instructors who will teach art than painters who will paint pictures. Based as it is on a single painting style, it is necessarily somewhat one-sided. To develop an original style, a painter needs a more general training than this, the larger flexibility and facility that only a complete schooling in drawing and painting will give. If the student intends to be a professional painter and needs more drawing than he can get at the universities, he can usually find it elsewhere. There are always the professional art schools. These, however, have been much influenced by the teaching methods used in the universities. Even the New York Art Students League, which has no connection with any system of educational standards, holds no examinations and gives no credits, and, consequently, has no reason to be anything but a place where people learn to paint, has yielded to the prestige of Modern Art. It now teaches painting by the same methods of compositional analysis that have found such favor in the universities, although a serious student will generally take a "conservative" course, a course in drawing, in one of his periods as a corrective measure. Professional art schools such as this are vastly more efficient than the universities in training painters. The Modern Art instruction at the League is so efficacious and the work turned out often so brilliant that the pictures in the students' exhibitions are frequently indistinguishable from the work of their professional elders housed farther east on Fifty-Seventh Street.

It can scarcely be held against this method of instruction that the students learn to paint brilliantly. The serious objection is that they learn to paint backwards. It considers that the basic qualities characteristic of a work of art are perfection of form, color and composition, and that by adding all these qualities together, a work of art can be produced which will hold the attention and be remembered. This is exactly the reverse of the accepted way of going about making a picture. Hitherto, a picture has usually been started with a visual idea which generates its own composition—from the inside out, so to speak. But the present system of Modern Art instruction teaches that a picture is best made as a composition which generates its own content, and from the outside in. The student who follows this method is in danger of becoming involved in all sorts of stylizations, archaisms, and direct imitations which he would otherwise avoid.

In fact, this system of painting is not unlike the eclectic school of the late Renaissance—Guido Reni, Vasari, Annibale Carracci and the others, who by joining the violence of Michelangelo to the sweetness of Raphael and the subtlety of Da Vinci, thought to arrive at perfect art—a perfection to be judged not on their pictures' own expressive qualities, but on how clearly the painters had reproduced the qualities of this composite model. The present-day system forgets, just as did the Eclectics, that what holds the attention in the long run is not a picture's perfection of form or purity of style. These are only devices for emphasis. What makes us continue to remember and to love a picture is its actual poetry, the human power of the visual ideas it conveys. Pictures executed in the strict canons of the style of Modern Art, in spite of its promise of modernity and show of violence, will in the end appear as sweet and vapid as the pictures of the Eclectics, or, for that matter, those of the Pre-Raphaelite Brotherhood.

Yet all this is of very little importance. No one ever follows the strict precepts of his painting instruction for very long after he has learned to paint. And Modern Art instruction is an admirable method of making clear to the student some of the most serious problems a painter has to solve. It would be a perfect method for teaching painting if pure composition were destined to remain the subject matter of our painting. But this cannot be. The three unities of Modern Art are no longer systematically observed by our contemporary painters; they have not been so observed for almost two decades. Moreover, the very fact that Modern Art can be thus competently taught shows that it is no longer modern. It is too well understood to hold much longer the attention of even those painters who still today obey its rules.

Any system of art instruction as complete as this is properly an academy. It is indeed very like the academy of Impressionism which furnished the best painting instruction thirty years ago. It might be called the academy of Cubism, except that the strict classical Cubism of the early Braques and Picassos is the one aspect of the Modern movement it never imitates. Besides this, the Modern academy does not seem to stem directly from the Modern masters themselves. It is too recent for that. It only appeared in this country around 1935, some twenty-odd years after Modern Art itself. The great influence it possesses today would seem to come from the prestige of the institutions where Modern Art is preserved and from the prestige of the universities which had begun shortly before the beginning of the Second World War to adapt the discoveries of the Modern masters to their courses of instruction. From these the Modern academy derived its present importance, its official tone and air of self-satisfaction. Recently it has acquired a dogmatic intolerance that Modern Art itself did not display at the time of its greatest expansion.

The painters themselves, for the most part, are a little wary of making an open break with official Modern Art. They have only to look in the pages of the *International Studio* of the early years of the century before the influence of Modern Art appeared, or into the pages of a present-day Soviet art magazine whence these influences have been excluded, to discover the vasty deserts from which our painting has escaped. Defection from the cause of Modern Art would seem to put a painter into the position of defending all the official painting of the past he most despises, even the anecdotal painting from which Impressionism saved us. But Modern Art needs no such allegiance. Its cause is won. What needs defense is the painter's right to secede from all official painting. And Modern Art is the official painting of today.

CHAPTER ELEVEN

ART AND ECONOMICS

Phonograph One: I have brought you to the Eiffel Tower to show you, before anyone else, a unique work of art—*The Wedding*
Phonograph Two: Who did it?
Phonograph One: What do you mean, who did it? It is one of the most recent works of God.
Phonograph Two: Is it signed?
Phonograph One: God never signs.
Jean Cocteau, *Les Mariés de la Tour Eiffel.*

Looking at pictures as we have been doing from the standpoint of the artist at work—looking at them as examples of what a painter of a given time had been able to accomplish—tends to deprive the pictures of their glamour and reduce them to human size and fallibility. But when we see the pictures themselves, framed by museums and ripened by time, they are vastly more imposing. Here they are public monuments and counsels of perfection. They are not mere paintings, they are art, leading lives of their own, independent of their authors.

The life of a picture as a work of art has no connection whatsoever with the social personality of the painter. It has nothing to do with his public behavior, his personal charm, his drawing-room manner. It derives instead from his most secret self, from his character as a man alone before his work. The writer's work is perhaps the direct extension of his personality; the painter's, never. Reading the writings of a friend one often says, "I can almost hear him talk." But no one, looking at a picture, can possibly say, "I can almost see him paint." The art of the painter is too private for this, so private as to seem a skill of hand rather than what it really is, a skill of mind. The painter is putting down a version of the world that can be expressed in no other terms than by his brush—a private landscape whose topography the painter's public presence does little to suggest. It is not of the slightest importance today that Raphael was a lady killer, Whistler a dandy, or Degas an old crab. These characteristics may have had considerable influence on the painters' choice of subject and on the formation of their styles. Today their only importance is to furnish art historians with anecdotes.

This is precisely the difference between painting and art; that art no longer belongs to the painter and the painter has no longer any part in it. This independent existence is what constitutes style, and style means, here, carrying power—the quality that makes a picture stick in one's mind. It is the continued vigor of this independent existence which keeps the picture on the museum's walls and out of the museum's cellar. It was the promise of such an independent existence which tempted the first purchaser to remove the picture from the painter's studio. The very fact that anyone should be moved to buy a picture proves that its ideas and execution are clear to others aside from the painter himself, that the picture has a possible existence in minds other than the painter's own. So, buying a picture and getting it away from the painter is the first step in turning a painting into art. And a work of art can almost be defined as a picture some painter has sold.

Thus, selling pictures is of enormous and real importance to the painter. It is sometimes a great deal more difficult for him even than painting them, for the pictures he turns out are a series of unique objects and generally quite expensive. These objects, if not necessarily intended to be privately owned, are nevertheless intended to be privately enjoyed; even more so today since modern pictures, on account of the private nature of the painter's subject matter, are suited almost exclusively to private uses. But no painting since the sixteenth century has ever had an appeal for a group audience. Hand-painted pictures arouse in their beholders no sentiments which are intensified because they are shared such as the play, the moving picture or the symphony orchestra evoke. On the contrary, a hand-painted picture speaks to only one man at a time. Even as few as two picture lovers standing in front of the same picture may seriously annoy each other.

Besides, the picture exists in only one copy. Unlike the book, it cannot be multiplied. The processes of color reproduction may eventually be perfected. At the present time color prints are feeble replicas, nowhere nearly as effective in communicating the spirit of a work as phonograph records, for example. Moreover, the processes of color printing are difficult and expensive. Reproductions can be made of only a very small class of pictures indeed—those which are already celebrated. At best, color prints can serve only to remind people of the pictures they already know. Under special conditions, a group of a painter's similar pictures—like Corot's nymphs or Monet's water lilies—may act as multiplications of the same picture, so that more people will see it. But this is necessarily a multiplication by a very small factor; even in this case the number of people who can be put in the presence of the painter's picture is extremely limited. Consequently, if the painter today is to depend on the simple inspection of his work to spread his fame, if he must wait for accident to place in front of his work the particular person who is capable of loving it, the painter's fame will be slow to spread.

Formerly this was easier. The painter's world was smaller. The painter lived in a middle-sized town like Florence or Siena or Toledo, as did Giotto or Simone or Greco, or worked for a social set all of whose members knew one another, as did Van Dyke or Holbein, or was painter to a royal court, like Velasquez or Clouet. Under these conditions, anyone who was interested in pictures could find out as soon as it had happened what sort of painting was generally available, what sort of work a particular painter was doing and what he was capable of.

But the great painting successes of our own time have had a broader field. They have been built on an international and not on a local market. The painter's public is spread out wide and thin. People with a common taste in painting are scattered all over the world. Communication between painter and client, among the clients themselves, and even among painters, is becoming increasingly difficult. As a consequence, there is usually a considerable lag today between the time a painter perfects a style and the moment when his pictures reach their eventual public.

The great painting successes of immediately before and after the First World War—of Braque, Picasso, Matisse, Duchamp, and so on—were made by using the most advanced techniques of modern advertising to shorten this too long gap between the production and the consumption of painting. The production was concentrated in Paris; the sale and distribution of the pictures controlled by a small group. This consisted of merchants who had Modern pictures to sell, and poets and literary men who knew how to influence the literary world; which was considered the sole possible market for advanced painting. The merchants were Sagot-Clovis, Vollard, Madame Weil, Kahnweiller, Paul Rosenberg, Paul Guillaume, Bignou, Drouet and a few others. The principal poets were first Apollinaire, later Cocteau, and at length, Eluard. The operation was so successful that almost no time at all after the Modern painters had begun to paint, their work was known to the entire world.

The same sort of publicity was used to promote music. The ballet itself became a showcase to display new composers along with the new painters. Cocteau advertised Eric Satie by enclosing him in a presentation package along with Picasso and the Ballet Russe, and carried out a masterful campaign for five French composers—Milhaud, Auric, Honegger (who is Swiss), Poulenc, and Germaine Taillefere, under the somewhat misleading title of *Les Six*. Ezra Pound tried to apply the same promotion methods to the American composer, George Antheil, but with too heavy or too inexperienced a hand. The publicity backfired, deprived Antheil of his public, and almost stopped his career.

High pressure publicity like this is not without its dangers to the artist. The first of these dangers is that the publicity may not work. It may reach the wrong public. Newspapers, popular magazines, radio and television are useful and necessary for publicizing the popular arts and the art works which are issued in multiple copies—movies, books, music and the theatre. But popular advertising is worse than useless for selling the painter's pictures which come in editions of one. The painter's success must be started in that small group of people who have both a taste for collecting and a real visual sensitivity. These people are individualists, highly resistant to the popular forms of advertising and most easily offended. These are the people most difficult to coerce by a campaign of publicity. Yet, until the confidence of this nucleus has been acquired, the painter's fame cannot begin to grow beyond his local circumstances. And in this case, I am afraid, the well-known maxim of advertising will not work. If you tell it to Sweeney, the Rockefellers will let you strictly alone.

Publicity's second danger for the painter is even greater. It is that the publicity campaign may succeed. A too sudden or too early fame may easily overwhelm the painter and neutralize his talent. ("Thank God," says John Sloan, "I never had success before fifty.") And the fame obtained through high pressure publicity is the most sudden and, to the painter, the most dangerous of all. This is natural enough. Publicity is a modern use of the old principles of applied magic. It consists, like magic, of incantation. In its effect it is no way different from the adept's invocation of a succubus. This elemental, according to the grimoires, is easy enough to summon, pleasant to have around and quite fun to use. But it has one drawback. It is likely to leave you dead on the floor one morning with your head snatched round. This, in our time, has happened to many promising painters.

I have always suspected that our century's taste for naïve painting was willfully engineered and artificially established by these same poets and press agents. For normally, naïve painting has little interest for the painter, the tradition of painting, or for the picture collector either. Anything that is art—that is to say, anything that can be looked at again and again, that holds the attention and can be remembered—and still appears to be naïve (like Abyssinian painting or thirteenth century stained glass) is simply an art done in an unfamiliar tradition, in a language, so to speak, whose grammatical structure differs from our own. It is not naïve at all, and in spite of the theories of child education now fashionable in our progressive schools, nobody but energetic and sophisticated men could possibly have produced it. But the naïve painters famous today—Bauchant, Grandma Moses, and so on—are for the most part undeniably naïve. They charm rather than interest. They evoke the spectator's condescension rather than his surprise. They exhibit no new image of the world. They exploit only the lowest common denominator of the visual memory, and the commonplaces of what is known as the "realistic" (in other words, the meticulous) painting style. Consequently, they belong only to the history of picture collecting, and not to the tradition of painting.

These naïve painters depict their residual memories of the world as it appears to a child. They count rather than see; this is the reason for their painful attention to detail—the number of bricks in a wall, the number of leaves on a tree. Many of them in the end acquire a greater skill in putting down their paint, or a greater charm of color than the common run. But for the most part, these naïve painters are all alike. Their style is international. It is impossible to tell one of them from another. The naïve painters I have mentioned differ from thousands of other self-taught painters who also paint on Sunday only by the fact that these particular painters have been publicized. This sort of painting, celebrated as some of it may be, and charming as it undoubtedly is when one happens upon it by accident, is nevertheless of no interest whatsoever to the professional painter. Nor would it be of interest to the picture collector either, except for the publicity value artificially attached to the painter's name.

The first and most celebrated of them all, the Douanier Rousseau, was discovered by Alfred Jarry. That in itself is suspicious. Jarry, author of *Ubu Roi*, *Le Surmâle*, and other farcical extravaganzas, was one of the most outrageous practical jokers of his time. And Rousseau's comic and engaging innocence made him a perfect butt for horseplay. Jarry introduced Rousseau to Apollinaire, the press-agent-in-chief of the Cubist painters. Rousseau's subsequent fame is exactly the sort of elephantine practical joke that Jarry, abetted by Apollinaire, would have been capable of perpetrating: starting with a charming goof and some pictures in the common Sunday manner, to create a great painter and impose his pictures on the market.

Rousseau's small pictures are like all other pictures by naïve painters, though it must be admitted that his large canvases have great style. In his *Sleeping Gipsy*, at the Museum of Modern Art of New York, the recumbent figure with its candy-striped robes and flattened face, the mandolin and the water jug have a sophistication in their distortions curiously reminiscent of Picasso himself. His jungles with their enormous leaves are impossible to forget. But this is not surprising. Style and carrying power are not always absent from the naïve painters' work. The residual memories of childhood they evoke command a sort of recognition in us all. And it is the possession of styles such as this which has permitted Rousseau's work to be so widely publicized.

The work of the amateur painter, on the other hand, can not be publicized. The amateur has not the narrow approach to painting of the naïve painter. His work lacks the carrying power the naïve painter often has. The amateur painter is in general an educated man whose main professional interests lie in some other field. Many doctors, actors, statesmen and others paint extremely well. Their pictures are frequently very good indeed, lively, interesting and well constructed. They can give great pleasure hanging on a wall; as hand-work, they are more entertaining and wear better than the finest reproductions. But it is only on account of some extraordinary success in his own profession, and not on account of the quality of the pictures themselves, that the amateur painter (like Churchill, Hitler or

Mendelssohn) can ever become known to the world at large. For the distinguishing mark of the amateur is his lack of original ideas. His proper originality and his principal strength he reserves for his own profession. Talented and skillful as his painting may be, it will nevertheless be adopted from some painter or some school of painting he admires. His painting style cannot be one that he himself has developed. He has not time for the painful and minute exploration of the visible world that the professional spends all his life learning to do. The amateur may be a man of talent. But real painting is not done on talent. Real painting is the expression of visual ideas—as Leonardo said, "una cosa mentale," a thing of the mind. Anyone can have talent. Talent is only the grease that helps the wheels go round. But if the painter has somewhere to go, he can creak along perfectly well without it.

The great Modern masters were never naïve. Nor were they amateurs. They were men of profoundly original and effective visual ideas, as well as being both trained and talented painters. The work of Picasso, Braque, Duchamp, Klee, and the rest, is of as high a quality and of as great a carrying power as the work of Monet or Manet, or, for that matter, of Ingres and David. It is to the real carrying power of their painting that they owe their present-day position in the world of art. I do not believe, however, that a painter of today, even if he possesses all these painters' gifts, could reproduce their success or their careers. Careers such as these cannot be made without publicity. And the contemporary painter has little effective publicity machinery at his service.

The great Modern painters themselves, in spite of their

early and world-wide fame, have always had a limited buying public for their pictures. They were exploring a private and professional world, fascinating to the painters themselves, but too hermetic to convince a broad public. The only audience that understood their pictures' content was the small inner circle of friends and poets who were amused by the painters' problems. This was a literary public, more sensitive to the intellectual abstractions of poetry than to the more concrete sensualities of painting. It is the character of this public which helps explain the otherwise puzzling over-simplifications found in certain of these Modern pictures. The painters were reducing the normal complexities of painting to make it clear to minds principally trained in the use of words.

Minds such as these, however, are the best press agents. By their help, the great public has at length accepted Modern Art. The style itself has been popularized in decoration, advertising and industrial design. Today the standard reproductions of the works of the masters and their immediate predecessors are to be found in any home of intellectual pretension, but the sale of original pictures has not increased. Rather it seems to have diminished. Museums, it is true, constantly acquire new examples of the Modern masters and of the better-known younger painters. But here in this country at any rate, there is little new buying by private collectors of any contemporary painting, Modern or otherwise. The great public that used to buy painting does not invest in the Modern school; this public does not yet understand the pictures and finds them difficult to hang. Because of the intellectual prestige that Modern Art commands, this public hesitates to compromise itself by buying the pictures which it finds intelligible. The smaller public which understands and likes Modern Art hesitates to acquire pictures by the younger Modern painters because it knows no canons of taste to distinguish the valuable and professional work of the school from the work of students and amateurs. Besides, the shock value of Modern Art has diminished. No war need any longer be waged in its defense. We approve of it as a cause. We no longer feel any obligation to invest in its pictures.

To add to the painter's difficulty, painting has no longer any effective central meeting place where opinions can be compared and tastes can be formed, such as Venice, Florence and Paris once were. Paris today seems very quiet and is directing our contemporary taste hardly at all. New York is a musical rather than a painting center. Except for architecture, it has never shown anything but a docile and provincial taste in the visual arts. For the contemporary painter, if he is a non-conformist, there exists little outside help of any sort for his career or for his pictures. The set-up originally organized for the distribution of Modern Art is still there. But this serves to distribute only those pictures painted in a recognizable Modern style. This publicity set-up is very like a railroad line. It is impossible to use it to go anywhere except where the roadbed leads. Painters wishing to visit other places can scarcely take it. And since it is best adapted for carrying large, impressive and public canvases to distant markets, the painters of smaller and more personal pictures may not find reservations.

This publicity machinery in this country today consists principally of the exhibition of contemporary painting by the museums, and the reporting of these exhibitions by the art magazines. The exhibition halls are large. They hold many pictures. The painters, naturally enough, send their largest pictures, and those that have the greatest carrying power. The judges wish to select the pictures according to carrying power. But carrying power is the picture's power to stick in the memory, not to be seen at a distance. This quality of being memorable is impossible to estimate at first sight, so that the pictures are generally selected on what the judges can mistake for carrying power, which is visibility.

As a result, the contemporary pictures in the museum exhibitions are invariably well painted, large and visible. They are pictures designed to command the eye. They are made out of the most brilliant and the most public materials, not the most personal. They resemble either posters, fabric designs or short stories. They are eminently suited to museum purchase. They are almost always too noisy to hang in a private home. The more brilliant, interesting and successful the museum's exhibition of contemporary painting, the less the private purchaser finds to buy.

Nevertheless, without the private purchaser our painting could not exist. The history of painting since the death of Ingres has been the history of the work of the painters who did not conform. These have always been supported by private purchase. Government or official purchase has always come later after they were famous or well established, frequently after they were dead. Nor can this be otherwise. In the international world of industry which came into existence with our railroad systems, local fame is not enough to sell a product. And advanced painting has this disadvantage: it is a local product and a one-man job, and cannot be industrialized.

In fact, painting is the last of the one-man hand techniques to survive in the modern world. In a large world such as ours, where wealth is perhaps more broadly and more evenly distributed than ever before, handmade objects have become too expensive to use. Their actual manufacture by hand is perhaps cheap enough. Things like clothes and shoes can still be made better and cheaper by hand than by machinery. But these handmade objects must be turned out one by one, each designed for a particular client. However cheaply each one can be made, when it comes to organizing this sort of unit manufacture under large scale industrial conditions, advertising the product, and distributing it, one by one, to a widespread market, the cost becomes prohibitive. This is exactly the case of the hand-painted picture. Here in America today, by the time an ordinary man has become acquainted with a painter's pictures through the conventional operations of publicity, the prices are already too high for him to think of affording one. The only way he can hope to buy a picture is by being a personal friend of a painter.

This is not the way that pictures are collected in Europe, and for a very simple reason. In Europe, money spent for pictures comes out of the collector's capital, whereas in America, pictures are bought out of income. In fact, in Europe, with its traditional insecurity of currency, it is only pictures, books, stamp collections, furniture, land, houses and so on, that can be considered capital, or used as currency. Buying things like these is considered a proper capital investment. A picture collector will buy, cheap and early, pictures by all the contemporary painters he has reason to trust and will then wait for a rise in prices. After a short time he will be able to find out, by living with the pictures, which of them have carrying power, and by watching the market, which will go up in value. The others he will trade in. After ten or fifteen years he will be the possessor of a valuable collection of pictures, and of a considerable capital as well. Because, in Europe, such a collection can always be sold for a profit, no matter what happens to the currency.

As an example, there is a story about a French family that owned a set of Louis XVI furniture. When the war took away their income, they sold the furniture, replaced it by a set of Empire, and lived for a year on the difference. In the meantime, Empire furniture had gone up in price, so they sold the Empire and replaced it with Louis Philippe. The Louis Philippe then went up, and if they had needed to, they could then have sold the Louis Philippe and bought Napoleon III. But by this time the war was over. Many Europeans did exactly the same with their pictures.

The prices in transactions such as these are governed by what similar objects are bringing at the public auctions. The prices of old pictures are regulated by the public sales at Christie's in London, and those of modern pictures by the sales at the Salle des Ventes in Paris, although the smooth operation of both of these markets has been somewhat interrupted by the complications of the after-war.

In America, however, no such stock market exists. Prices of furniture in public auction are governed, not by the value of the pieces themselves, but by the needs of the interior decorators. A bad example of something a fashionable decorator has brought into style will bring a fantastic price. A good example of something the decorators have not thought of using will go for nothing, all this quite independent of the piece's intrinsic value. As for pictures, since the decorators do not use them, no such market exists at all. On account of our system of taxation and of the high cost of ordinary living, pictures are more expensive to paint here than abroad. And because in matters of painting we are a provincial country, with all the timidity of provincial taste, our picture collectors hesitate to invest in pictures which have not already received critical approval; in other words, pictures whose prices are already high. Pictures bought at such price levels—and not on a rising market—can seldom be resold without considerable loss. Consequently, in this country a picture is almost always bought out of the collector's income, like an automobile, with the expectation either of using it up oneself, or if it is later to be sold, of selling it with a considerable mark-down for depreciation.

Even our museums do not buy pictures out of capital. Nor do they consider as capital the pictures they own. Their capital is the stocks and bonds and real estate of their endowment. It is from the income of these—or from the money that they get by the sale of pictures they inherit and do not wish to keep—that all their new pictures are bought. Nobody but the poor and the professional classes has more income than capital. So, in America, it is not the rich, it is the painter's poor friends who buy his pictures.

For this situation there is at the moment no remedy. Also there is nobody to blame. It is principally that the painter is a solitary workman, and as such—temporarily perhaps—does not fit into the industrial set-up of the contemporary world. The musicians and the composers of music have the phonograph, the films, radio and television, to furnish them with an audience, to utilize their talents and sustain their prestige. Writers have behind them the forces of education and the literacy of the present-day world. The scientists and technicians live protected in the monastic seclusion of company laboratories—perhaps less secluded today—and communicate with one another in our present-day equivalent of medieval Latin, the international language of mathematics. The painter alone of all the intellectual workmen is unemployable, except perhaps as teacher.

Most probably this awkward exclusion will not last. Even today, the painter is not as badly off as the serious composers were twenty years ago, and today the music of the contemporary composers has a large and increasing audience. The painter's situation may also change, and just as unexpectedly. But for the moment he will have to console himself with Degas' irony, "In my time, Sir, one did not succeed"—"De mon temps on n'arrivait pas"—and stick it out as well as he can. And stick it out he will. Because hand painting is one of the most satisfactory things in the world. Writing books is sad labor, and writing music is putting down directions for what some other man must do. But the painter has all the joys of immediate creation, his picture, like Adam, coming to life under his hand.

CHAPTER TWELVE

PAINTING TODAY

What is your attitude toward art today?
I like to look at it.

Answer by Gertrude Stein to a questionnaire in *The Little Review*. May, 1929.

For the painter who wants to make composition the real subject of his picture, what the picture represents is just an obstacle; in fact it is the major obstacle. If the picture's composition is to have its proper emphasis, all reference to the familiar visual world must be destroyed. Or if this is too drastic, the objective meaning of the image it presents must at least be considerably weakened. Otherwise the painter is just where he was before, painting a picture which is well composed perhaps, but which is still an anecdote, an illustration. This difficulty the Modern artists avoided by their most brilliant device—the multiple image, or the visual pun. By multiplying meaning, by making a picture with layers of images or layers of meaning, the value of each image can be weakened, and the mind can be drawn from the picture's sense to the picture's composition.

This is Modern Art's greatest originality, and it is the systematic employment of the multiple image, of the visual pun, which distinguishes Modern Art from all preceding painting. The multiple image is the prime necessity of any Modern or contemporary picture. Its presence in any picture immediately renders that picture acceptable to contemporary taste. It is the one form of decorative richness our century admits—the ornamentation in depth.

For us in our time, if a thing is to hold the attention, one plane of existence, one level of meaning, is no longer enough. A thing must mean two or three things at the same time. By these extra meanings, it acquires for us the depth, the back-and-forth dimension, the uncertain position, and the evasive essence which, for us, all real existence has. It is these multiple meanings which render a thing interesting to us and keep it so, whether it be an opera of Mozart or a character in Proust.

The double image in itself is nothing new. The drawings which illustrate the literature of alchemy are all double images, a secret language whose meaning is today perhaps utterly lost. Allegory, which was the subject matter of so much of the painting and poetry of the Middle Ages and of the Renaissance, is but the systematic use of double images. Decorative painters, like the sixteenth century Arcimboldo, for example, often painted landscapes, or still-lifes, which seen from a certain distance became grotesque faces. But here the double image was only a decoration or a joke; or, as with the alchemists, was used to conceal knowledge in an impressive and secret alphabet; or, as in allegory, furnished the painter with a useful framework for composing the world he knew into large, rich pictures, at the same time exhibiting his philosophy or his wit.

But the double image employed by Modern Art is none of these things. It is neither a secret meaning nor an allegory. It does not use one meaning to conceal another. All its meanings are equally important. It fails of its purpose if it becomes either jocular or merely decorative. It is so characteristic of our time that it is almost impossible for the contemporary artist to be inspired to work without it. We all know how the Gothic stonecutters kept themselves interested in their work, which otherwise would have become stiff and solemn, by playing little practical jokes upon it—by placing mocking figures concealed behind the figures of the Virtues, or by teasing the saints with some indignity only the craftsman knew was there. In the same way, the painter of our time keeps himself interested in his work and keeps his work alive by giving his pictures an extra meaning and a double take.

The first examples I know of this, although there are undoubtedly others, are in Manet's *Olympia* and in his *Déjeuner sur l'Herbe*. These are pictures of contemporary people in contemporary, if somewhat scandalous, settings, and painted in one of the most advanced of the contemporary painting styles. They are at the same time accurate parodies of celebrated older pictures. So that the subject of Manet's pictures is in reality the double image, *Then and Now*, done with extraordinary skill, dash and finish.

Double images like this do not exist in the Impressionists. Cézanne's bathers are not parodies of Rubens; they are the thing itself. Renoir may remind one of Boucher, but only because both like pink and white girls. Van Gogh's copies of Millet and Delacroix are exactly what they pretend to be, carefully executed copies whose only strangeness was their up-to-date brush work and tonality. But for us, the parody, the visual pun, the multiple image, is an essential part of all our serious art—our poetry, our music and our painting. It is characteristic of our humor—the joke where the situation given by the drawing is contradicted by the social situation implied by the one-line caption. This multiple image made of terms of equal weight has been the distinguishing mark of every picture that has held our attention since the first appearance of Modern Art, from Picasso's pink period parodies of the nudes of Puvis de Chavannes; through the kaleidoscope of double images in the *Nude Descending a Staircase;* through the Italian Futurists and their attempts to portray by multiple images the appearance of motion; through the actual superposed and frequently dissimilar images of the Surrealists, of Dali and Max Ernst; through the more subtle double images of the Neo-Romantics, of Bérard, Tchelitchew, Leonid and Berman—the image of the personality of the painter reflected in the character of the thing seen; down to the carefully inconsequential titles attached for the purpose of evoking a double image to the abstract pictures of the Modern academy.

The most fecund, perhaps, of the methods for producing a double image the Modern painters found in the analysis of painting styles. Such analysis of style is what is generally known in music as Neo-Classicism. The same sort of analysis of other styles is also used in painting. The meaning of the picture, no matter what it is a picture of, can thus be modified, or even contradicted, by its more general meaning. It becomes a picture of a thing and at the same time the picture of a style. Neo-Classicism, however, in painting as in music, runs this danger: the painter must beware of a too great admiration for the style he takes as model. Otherwise he will be led to imitate its mannerisms, and will end, as did David and the Pre-Raphaelites, in sentimental archaisms and scholarly redundancies. If his picture is to be a successful double image, it must evoke the stylistic and compositional devices of a school, and not the details of its painting. In this sort of stylistic analysis Braque and Picasso were not the first. Whistler's *Mother*, for example, does the same. It is more than a picture of a dear little old lady. It is also a serious exposition of the Japanese system of space-filling by occult balance and rectangular composition. Whistler's *Mother*, nevertheless, is not a Modern picture; the meaning of the image is still the meaning of the picture. In a Modern picture, the importance of the meaning of such an image would have been reduced. The important thing is instead the duality—the image itself contrasted to its use as a framework on which to display the essential elements of a style.

For a Neo-Classicism such as this, all styles are not equally suitable. The style selected must be old enough or far enough away to be visible to us as a definite and foreign style. Thereupon, the shock of the double image comes from the incongruity of the content and its clothing. This, for example, is the Neo-Classicism of Stravinsky's *Concerto for Piano and Wind Orchestra*, where a modern rhythmic system is dressed in an elaboration of early eighteenth century counterpoint; of Picasso's *Mother and Child*, where a family portrait is disguised as a late Roman fresco;

of the same painter's costumes for Satie's ballet *Parade*, where the ineffectual managers are clothed in the monumental style of a New York skyscraper; of Milhaud's early tangos, written to sound as if they were being played on an out-of-tune piano in a Brazilian dive; of the films of Mae West, where an up-to-date and brazen sexuality is displayed in the rococo trappings of a decade supposed to be more prudish than our own.

The real difficulty about this sort of Neo-Classical double image is that it is ephemeral. It loses its shock and most of its interest as soon as the style of the piece itself becomes identified in the public's mind with the exotic or historic style the piece has set out to evoke. This can happen after a very short time indeed. Already today, Stravinsky's dissonant counterpoint sounds like a richer form of Handel. Picasso's *Mother and Child* looks like a careful art school drawing. The public is now coming to be convinced that the 90's were really naughty. Thus, the double image given by Neo-Classicism is extremely fragile. When it works, it works only for a public that has been educated to understand the joke. It is very useful for introducing a work of art to an intellectual public, but after the Neo-Classical references have worn off, the picture must depend for our continued interest on itself. In fact, it is only at this point, when the double image due to recondite stylistic references has disappeared, that the Neo-Classic work can escape from the snob public and be taken up by the public at large.

Essentially, however, it is composition, not the double image, which is the subject of the Modern picture. The visual pun, the multiple image, is only one device for weakening the image's importance and thus focusing the attention on the picture's composition. There is another device for this which is equally effective—painting pictures that have no recognizable images at all.

A recognizable image, an image that is the representation of something in the outside world, is not, in spite of common popular opinion, a necessary part of a picture. A picture in its simplest terms is something that fills a space—whether on a wall or on a piece of paper—and can hold a spectator's attention. If the attention can be held without the use of an image, and if the painter can be inspired to work without an image to elaborate, the image is unnecessary. The absence of an image should even serve to make the act of painting less laborious. Hence, the abstract picture.

The absence of the image has, nevertheless, certain disadvantages for the painter. As I have pointed out, the Modern painter was persuaded to take composition as his subject matter largely on account of the, to him, abstract character of savage and exotic art. He could feel the force of the forms and shapes this art contained without having any notion of the meanings or even of the precise images they were intended to convey. Such meanings did exist for the artists themselves who made this exotic art. It was precisely these meanings which generated the forms and shapes the Modern painter found so interesting. Shapes such as these, put on the painter's canvas for purely formal and stylistic reasons, without an image or a meaning to animate them, will be unlikely to generate such power. The painter is saying to his lines and shapes, not "say this for me," but only "be beautiful and moving." He has only his imagination to depend on to give them richness and variety. The human imagination, separated from the variety and richness of the world outside the mind, with only itself to work on, is surprisingly dull. The imagination operates, not by creating new forms, but by rearranging old symbols. These symbols take on warmth and amplitude only when they are quickened by some contact with the outside world. So, the abstract painter, with only his unaided imagination to give his lines and shapes variety, will paint thin pictures. There is more possibility for richness in a discipline of accident—making accidental spots and choosing the most interesting—or in the mathematical formula.

It has long been supposed, and I would not presume to deny it, that there lies behind all real beauty some simple mathematical relation. Certainly music, or at any rate harmony, is based on such an arithmetic, on the simple common fractions, the Pythagorean divisions of the stretched string which produce the musical intervals. It has been claimed, with considerable justification, that the perfection found in Greek art is due to the constant repetition in their proportions of the irrational ratios—one to the square root of two, of three and of five. It has been suggested that the composition of the Byzantine mosaics, of all medieval art, of all painting, in fact, down to the break-up of the guilds, was made possible by some simple mathematical rule of thumb, some lost trick of laying-out with string and rule and compass which gave these works their balance and their beauty.

Certainly, the iconography of the Middle Ages is full of number. One means God; two means man and God; three, the Trinity (hence, triple time is the only beat used in medieval music for serious compositions); four, the evangelists, and so on. Such simple numbering has still, even today, its uses in design. All painters, for example, are aware that a still-life comes out better with an odd number of objects. More than this, it is often claimed that by investigating the properties of number, and the mathematical relationship of shapes—the golden section, the distribution of the primes, the square, the cubical, the pyramidal numbers, and so on—that the painter can recover a complicated lost tradition, and with its aid, produce inevitable beauty.

But if some numerical system of composition once existed, it is more than doubtful that it could be recovered with only the painter's feelings for shape and proportion to guide him to it. Such research, however, has exercised many aestheticians and painters of our time. As used by the realistic painters, the results have been for the most part disappointing. Witness George Bellows's tiresome uses of the formulas of "Dynamic Symmetry"—his prize fight pictures (there is one in the Metropolitan Museum) where the arms and legs of the fighters follow the diagonals of the "whirling square" and point awkwardly to the corners of the frames. But for the abstract painter, such formulas can be extremely useful. A mathematical formula, even if the authentic formula for producing beauty has not been found, can be of enormous aid in putting into motion the abstract painter's sluggish imagination. A great many musicians to my knowledge, John Cage for one, and a great many painters, I suspect, make use of such mathematical formulas for composition—an accidental spot, or line, or group of notes, which by a numerical formula for repetition, is made to fill the painter's canvas or the composer's time. The use of formulas is not new. The sonnet, the canon, even the three unities and strict versification of the French seventeenth century dramatists, were, in their way, such formulas for composition. But in these examples, the formula was used only to mold and make neater the shape which contained the meaning; whereas, in modern usage, the picture's meaning is the shape itself, and the works produced by a pure numerical treatment are in danger of ending as empty and mechanical productions.

Most frequently, the artist's inner mind interferes and fills the shapes with unexpected meaning. This is likewise true of the painting disciplines which are based on the accidents of spots and drippings. These disciplines, in fact, depend on such expectation, for meaning is the most difficult thing to exclude from painting. Any circle is at once a sun or an orange, any dash a thorn and any star a rose. But powerful as these invader meanings may be, and however great an interest they may add, I am tempted to believe that these mathematical and accidental processes of composition are not the processes of art at all. They are instead the processes of magic and of incantation. The artist hopes to stumble on some hidden force by accident, or to evoke it by ritual. The end of these processes is to bewitch and to dominate the spectator, not to please and instruct him. If one distrusts the use of magic, one must distrust the process of mathematical composition especially. If the formula succeeds, much of its force is derived from disappointments and bitternesses deep within the artist's hidden mind. The left-hand source of this power the artist himself does not recognize. But the magic it performs is more likely to be gray or black than white and benevolent. If the miracle does not take place, if the artist's shapes are not filled with an effective magic, the final result of such formulas is only an elaborate, empty and ingenious structure, precious and amusing perhaps, but principally useful to inspire the commercial designer and the interior decorator.

Yet just such a mathematical formula for composition provided the first violation of the classical Modern unities of composition as subject, equalized surface, and improvisation. This has an historical importance, for it is by the various violations and rearrangements of these unities that all the painting subsequent to Modern Art has been produced.

The first of these violations led straight to Modern architecture. It was invented and elaborated by the German-Dutch, for the ideas of Modern Art had spread with unbelievable rapidity to the east. Already by 1911, Paul Klee had begun his characteristic work and Kandinsky was already painting his abstract "*Improvisations.*" Also in 1911, Mondrian did three pictures of a cherry tree in bloom, each increasingly abstract. The first was a naturalistic rendition in the Impressionist technique. The second was a simplification of the forms of the tree into a linear pattern which was still recognizable as an image of the tree. The third was an abstraction, a composition in line alone. Whereupon, Mondrian carried the processes of abstraction still further. He abandoned not only the image but the double image as well. He eschewed all lines but the straight, all directions but the vertical and horizontal, all differences of paint texture, and all colors except those with simple names like red, orange, black or white. These flat-colored rectangles he placed on his canvas with all the neat precision of a student in physics plotting out the results of an experiment. The placing of these spots does not seem to be the result of the artistic fancy. It has all the air of being arrived at by strict mathematical calculation, on some theory that beauty is the necessary result of some set of mathematical proportions (like the piece of sculpture by Pevsner in the Modern Museum called *A Developable Column* and which is, in actual fact, a mathematical figure —"a developable surface" being the mathematical name for any surface traced in space by the movement of a straight line). But whether or not Mondrian's pictures were planned by numerical analysis as one is tempted to believe, it still remains that these pictures are in no way improvisations. They are most carefully planned in advance. Thus, of the three unities of Modern Art, Mondrian abandoned free improvisation. He kept only composition as his subject matter, and reduced the surface tension of his pictures to its most elementary and impersonal form—to the mechanically perfect surface of an architect's floor plan.

On account of the neutral character of Mondrian's paint surface the lines and shapes do not depend for their effect on any particular skill of hand. They do not have even to be in paint. They can be executed in anything that is resistant—in wood, linoleum, in glass, in stone, in brick—in anything whose edges can be kept rectangular and neat. This depersonalization of painting proved to have great industrial value. It was of particular interest to the architect. It does not put too great a strain on the pocketbook of his clients, on the capabilities of his workmen, or on his own knowledge of drawing.

Architectural schools of the present day scarcely teach

free-hand drawing at all. The architect will indeed have learned in school how to draw a tree for his perspective rendering. But he will seldom have learned enough about drawing to be able to plan his building as a piece of sculpture, as a solid, space-occupying whole, in the way that the older architects, Bernini or Palladio for example, were accustomed to do. As a consequence of this undeveloped sense of space due to his lack of training in drawing, the architect of today is happiest when he can plan his building as an assemblage of rectangular flats, interlocking cubes, and cylinders, and can pretend to be less an artist than an engineer. This the aesthetic of Mondrian permits him to do.

In fact, this simplification of Modern Art turned out to be of such general industrial interest that as soon as it became possible after the First World War, a school was founded in Germany to teach its theories, the Bauhaus in Dessau, with Klee, Feininger, and the architect Gropius among its instructors. The school flourished until 1925 and its effects can still be seen. It was responsible for some of the finest architecture of our time, as well as for some of the least interesting, for its aesthetic of the flat, unornamented surface in rectangular shapes can be used, even today, as an excuse for all sorts of poverties—of materials, of detail, of imagination, and of design. Thus, the first rearrangement of the canons of Modern Art—abandoning the methods of improvisation and using a mechanical equivalent for equalized surface tension—produced both Modern architecture and the commercial forms of Modern Art.

A second kind of rearrangement of the canons began to be employed about 1924 by the painters connected with the French Surrealist movement. Among these were Dali, Miró, Magritte, Max Ernst, Tanguy, with Chirico as a precursor. The violation these painters practiced was a particularly interesting and fecund one. They abandoned composition as subject matter for their pictures and took instead of it the double image. With the classical Modern painters and their school, the double image had been only a device for weakening meaning so that composition could take its place as the real subject of the picture. But the Surrealist painters relegated composition to a second place; the subject matter of their pictures became the visual pun. Furthermore, their multiple and precise meanings were generally called to the spectator's attention by a provocative and surprising title attached to the picture as one of its necessary parts. *Children Menaced by a Nightingale* of Max Ernst—two children fleeing apparently from a cuckoo clock—or *The Survivor* of Magritte—a realistic picture of a rifle dripping with blood. Max Ernst, Tanguy and others retained the equalized surface and the methods of improvisation. Dali and Magritte abandoned even these, and painted their pictures in a pre-Impressionist style—Dali, in a manner derived from the style of the Italian tempera painters as reconstructed by the Pre-Raphaelites; Magritte in the half-naïve, half-commercial painting style found in sign boards and circus posters. Thus, by giving the pictures an air of candor, the shock of the multiple image could be intensified.

Surrealism and the visual pun have had in recent years considerable industrial and decorative application. Emilio Terry made some extraordinary architectural designs—

buildings in the shape of grottos or draped columns, but as far as I know none of them have yet been executed. A piece of furniture, designed by Dali, was built, and displayed—a sofa which was at the same time a pair of lipsticked lips. He has also executed a display at a world's fair, the sets and costumes for several ballets, and a *Madonna and Child.* Dali, in fact, is the only one of the Surrealist painters who has had a marked commercial success. In recent years the Dali style itself has been much imitated and even used in advertising. Today it seems to be disappearing, perhaps because the public is coming to know too well the Freudian system of symbols on which Dali's double images were based.

Herein lies the weakness of this painting. Its interest comes from its poetic rather than from its technical invention. The visual pun is a literary device, a poetic or anecdotal subject matter. As such its life is short. Once its references are commonly understood, it no longer holds our interest. The permanent interest of this painting must be judged apart from its subject matter, as any painting must be judged, on purely painting grounds. The pictures of Dali and Magritte are painted in a style that is a reaction against the Impressionists' discoveries. Although they are executed with extraordinary skill, finish, and even beauty of surface, they can scarcely be considered a technical advance. They are, instead, planned pictures, not unlike the academy pictures of the 80's and 90's, except that they have for subject a visual pun instead of a clear anecdote. This cannot be said of the painting of Miro or of Tanguy, who depend on the purest form of improvisation—on the discipline of spontaneity where the motion of the brush as well as the images it creates are derived from the subliminal mind.

A third kind of rearrangement of the Modern canons appeared in Paris in 1926 with the Neo-Romantic painters. These were principally Bérard, Tchelitchew, Leonid, and Eugène Berman. These painters kept the Modern methods of improvisation. But they replaced the equalized surface tension by an equalized, often penumbral, lighting of the subjects represented. Like the Surrealists, they substituted the double image for composition as the subject of their painting. But their double image was a very special kind. It became a double communication—that of the object depicted and the artist's feelings about it. It was this insistence on the painter's personal feelings which connected the Neo-Romantic painters with Romanticism. Bérard and Tchelitchew painted portraits which were portraits of real people and at the same time mirrors in which the painter's emotional preoccupations were reflected. Leonid and Eugène Berman made landscapes which were both real places and these same places seen through the private and distorting glasses of the painter's memory—either of the places themselves, or of the painter's memory of art.

Later, with the need of painting big pictures, and perhaps also through the influence of Surrealism, the scope of the Neo-Romantic double image was enlarged. Tchelitchew took on the double image of how people are also animals and how children in their growing belong to the vegetable world. Eugène Berman's pictures became pictures which were also ruins of pictures, or landscapes which were also stage sets or *objets d'art.* Bérard, led astray perhaps by his too perfect taste, spent much of his talent on costume and stage design. The finest pictures of these Neo-Romantics are for the most part in private collections, difficult to see and impossible to see together. Nevertheless, by reintroducing humanity and personal feelings into an art that had become dehumanized, the Neo-Romantic painters made, I am convinced, the most important contribution to painting since the innovations of the great Moderns, and one which will have much influence in forming the painting of the second half of our century.

The painters most in view in this country at the present moment are the young Abstractionists, the group which contains Jackson Pollock, Robert Motherwell, the late Arshile Gorky, and others. These painters derive from another sort of violation of the Modern unities. But the novelty of their work, whose chief influence seems to be Kandinsky, comes from a shift of emphasis rather than from a real innovation. With these painters, the surface tension of the painting, and not its composition, becomes the subject matter of their pictures. The paint is applied according to the strictest discipline of spontaneity, even sometimes according to a discipline of accident. But in spite of these painters' aspirations to modernity, the only thing systematically novel about these pictures is their large size. The painting methods employed are the standard Modern techniques, as these are practiced in the better art schools and colleges. The pictures themselves, which usually bear either a poetic title or an opus number, are striking principally for their elaborate surfaces produced by spattering, pouring and other standard methods of improvisation. The canvases are mostly quite large, so as to be as conspicuous as possible in exhibitions.

The attitude behind this art seems to be conservative. The chief element of surprise or shock about it is the fact that the painters themselves seem to believe that they are doing something new. But their very celebrity hints at the contrary. It is precisely the success of their work in official and academic circles that permits it to be distributed by the advertising machinery developed some thirty years ago for the use of Modern Art. A newer painting would not yet have such news value nor such a public.

So, contrary to what the abstract academy would tell us, this is not the whole painting of our time. It represents, I think, the end of something, rather than the rebirth of the heroic modernism it supposes itself to be. Its meager poetry and its loose construction seem to me inadequate to depict our human richness or our terrestrial adventure. Most certainly this is not the living tradition of painting in our day.

What any picture must possess to be actually of our time is some sort of double image, some added dimension of the imagination. This the painter of our time cannot avoid. Even when painting the most commonplace of objects, like Dali's loaf of bread, he must yet find in it some private meaning to hold his interest while he works, or to give his finished picture the wider importance of a symbol. Even the pictures produced by the strictest disciplines of accident or of systematic non-meaning must, to hold the spectator's attention, have the multiple meaning provided by a divergent title. But multiple meaning through words is the double image in its most evanescent form. A more fecund, a more varied, and a more permanent double image than this is offered by the simple duality of the mind and the outside world.

The external world we see and feel and hear is more varied than the world of our imagination. But the external world is only the world as it exists at the present moment. The world of the imagination is broader than this, for it has its existence in the past. It is made from the many external worlds of yesterday, shorn of their variety and reduced to the symbols our minds can handle. But however varied the world of nature may be, and however rich our memories of it, the interplay between the external world and the simplifications our minds impose on it is richer still. It is this interplay which provides the painter with the particular double image of which I speak, the difference between the interior, personal world which is of the past, and that mysterious land still outside the mind, which is the present.

Any fairly consistent system for reconciling these two divergent realities we call "realism." There have been many formulas for realism, because any system of depicting reality, no matter how convincing it may originally have been, remains accurate only for a limited time. By the time one of these systems has been accepted as the true picture of the outside world, both the outside world itself and our way of seeing it have already changed. The camera itself can provide a convincing representation of nature only for the particular age and civilization that invented it. Giotto, Gruenewald, Delacroix, Manet, Cézanne, were all attempting to produce a truer realism than their age afforded. But not one of their systems for depicting reality is capable of depicting the world a painter sees today. No past formula for "realism" can provide even a hint of the richness present before him.

Thus, a "realistic" painting style can never contain reality for any length of time. The real is contained only in the shifting relation of the mind to the world. Since the world and the mind which reflects it are both constantly in flux, the attempt to give an accurate representation of these two worlds is the most interesting, the most difficult, and consequently the most fruitful thing a painter can engage in. It is this ever-changing reality, this duality of the mind and the world which I believe to be the subject matter of the painter of today, and of the art of tomorrow.

For painting is prophetic, or at least it seems to be. The painter presents the world as he sees it when he paints. Everyone else sees the world as it was in the past, reflected in the retarding mirror of his memory. The painter painting a portrait is particularly aware of this. The family invariably complains that the sitter looks too old. This is quite natural. The sitter's family see only their memories of the sitter. Whereas the painter has depicted the sitter as he was at the moment when he was being painted, at a point the family's memories have not yet reached. In the same way, an official painting style is acceptable to everybody because it presents an image of the world that now exists in everybody's memory, and which, consequently, is now only an image of the past.

Thus, the world depicted by Modern Art is the world of an earlier part of our century, a world which the painter (like everyone else) was concerned in taking apart, perhaps because it had become too rigid to be lived in. Today we know what the parts are like. The problem now is how to assemble the pieces. The painter is also concerned with this. It cannot be solved by methods of abstraction, or by analyses of styles. We have looked at the shape of the pieces long enough. It is time now to reassemble them.

What the painter is searching for, and all the rest of us are too, is a world adapted to human sizes and to the shape of man. The painter of today is admirably equipped for his endeavor. He has an impressive heritage. He has available to him all the techniques of the planned picture, of the Impressionists, of organic composition, and even, if he needs its emphasis, of the poster. He has got rid of a great deal of unnecessary luggage. He has no longer the Impressionist's dependence on the theories of photography, although he knows the advantages of Impressionism's equalized surface and of its confidence in improvisation. He no longer needs Modern Art's subject of composition, but he still avails himself of all the richness the double image can provide. It is precisely these three things which characterize the living tradition of painting of our time—the equalized surface, improvisation, and multiplicity of meaning. These are the tools of our painting. They are not very different from the tools of Modern Art. But the painting of today has a different subject. It is not new. The painter has often used it before. The subject of our painting is no longer art, science, poetry, God, or mankind as a group. It is every individual man and the particular world that each inhabits. In short, the Grand Style.

INDEX

INDEX

INDEX

INDEX

INDEX

Modern Art:

171 picture's real subject is its own composition

181 child's drawing

196

204 talent

213 visual puns, layers of meaning 214 216

222 Invader meanings (Pollock) 227! 228 230